T3-BHM-331

NEW DIRECTIONS FOR TEACHING AND LEARNING

Robert J. Menges, *Northwestern University*
EDITOR-IN-CHIEF

Marilla D. Svinicki, *University of Texas, Austin*
ASSOCIATE EDITOR

Preparing Faculty for the New Conceptions of Scholarship

Laurie Richlin
Antioch College

EDITOR

Number 54, Summer 1993

JOSSEY-BASS PUBLISHERS
San Francisco

PREPARING FACULTY FOR THE NEW CONCEPTIONS OF SCHOLARSHIP
Laurie Richlin (ed.)
New Directions for Teaching and Learning, no. 54
Robert J. Menges, Editor-in-Chief
Marilla D. Svinicki, Associate Editor

Microfilm copies of issues and articles are available in 16mm and 35mm, as well as microfiche in 105mm, through University Microfilms Inc., 300 North Zeeb Road, Ann Arbor, Michigan 48106.

LC 85-644763   ISSN 0271-0633   ISBN 1-55542-726-X

NEW DIRECTIONS FOR TEACHING AND LEARNING is part of The Jossey-Bass Higher and Adult Education Series and is published quarterly by Jossey-Bass Inc., Publishers, 350 Sansome Street, San Francisco, California 94104-1310. Second-class postage paid at San Francisco, California, and at additional mailing offices. POSTMASTER: Send address changes to New Directions for Teaching and Learning, Jossey-Bass Inc., Publishers, 350 Sansome Street, San Francisco, California 94104-1310.

SUBSCRIPTIONS for 1993 cost $45.00 for individuals and $60.00 for institutions, agencies, and libraries.

EDITORIAL CORRESPONDENCE should be sent to Robert J. Menges, Northwestern University, Center for the Teaching Professions, 2003 Sheridan Road, Evanston, Illinois 60208-2610.

Cover photograph by Richard Blair/Color & Light © 1990.

 The paper used in this journal is acid-free and meets the strictest guidelines in the United States for recycled paper (50 percent recycled waste, including 10 percent post-consumer waste). Manufactured in the United States of America.

CONTENTS

EDITOR'S NOTES

Diversity in types of institutions has been one of the most notable characteristics of American colleges and universities. Since World War II, the
university research enterprise has exerted a centripetal force on virtually all
sectors of higher education, pulling their definition of success toward a
homogeneous focus on the discovery of new knowledge. Unfortunately, this
change has been at the expense of meeting the more individualized, local
needs of undergraduate education. The instruments of this change have
been the Doctors of Philosophy (Ph.D.'s), trained in specialized disciplinary
research and imbued with the research ethic, who bring their abilities and
preferences with them to faculty positions wherever they go. The on-the-job
activities of new faculty members call for knowledge and skills not inherent
to the standard Ph.D. program. In all fields, at all institutions, the greatest
need is for scholars to teach undergraduates. In contrast, the overwhelming
majority of American faculty never publish anything after their dissertation
material. This disparity between preparation and the need for faculty to be
able to teach to earn a living has been addressed, if at all, on a piecemeal
basis: patches of teaching experiences, internships in graduate programs,
and faculty development projects at employing institutions.

It is estimated that the graying of current faculty will require the
replacement of up to one-half million positions during the next few decades.
So, in addition to a need to develop appropriate preparation programs for
teacher-scholars, there also will be a need to recruit and prepare large
numbers of new academics. The aim of this volume, *Preparing Faculty for the
New Conceptions of Scholarship,* is to provide faculty and administrators with
both background information on current preparation efforts and an alternative framework for preparing the faculty of the future.

The chapters of this volume fall into three groups: traditional training
of the higher education faculty in the United States, their preparation for
scholarly work, and the future of these faculty. In Chapter One, I describe
how the increasing research orientation of graduate education since World
War II has moved the professoriate away from its original emphasis on
teaching. In Chapter Two, Judith S. Glazer reports the results of the attempt
to reform graduate education through the "invention" of the Doctor of Arts
degree. And, in Chapter Three, Jack H. Schuster places the responsibility for
preparing the new generation of faculty on the graduate school.

Chapters in the second group describe a broader view of faculty scholarship. In Chapter Four, I provide an overview of the four categories of
scholarship proposed by the Carnegie Foundation for the Advancement
of Teaching. Chapters Five through Eight address the implications of each
of these four categories for graduate education. In Chapter Five, Russell G.

Hamilton describes the multiple and varied forms of discovery research acceptable for dissertations. Muriel L. Blaisdell, in Chapter Six, advocates that graduate students go beyond disciplinary boundaries for academic integration. In Chapter Seven, R. Eugene Rice and I suggest that in many fields theory and practice are complementary, with each necessary for the enrichment of the other. And, in Chapter Eight, Shirley A. Ronkowski places the development of scholarly teaching into theoretical models and teaching-learning frameworks for educating and mentoring graduate students as future faculty.

The third group of chapters deals with the future of the U.S. faculty. The United States is becoming more diverse in many ways, including race, national origin, and language. In Chapter Nine, Trevor L. Chandler describes the importance of bringing into the professoriate as wide a range of experience as possible to reflect the increasing diversity of the student population. Finally, in Chapter Ten, I examine what Ph.D. programs (the providers of faculty) and hiring institutions (the consumers) will have to do in order to incorporate a broader conception of scholarship into the preparation of the faculty of the future.

Laurie Richlin
Editor

LAURIE RICHLIN is interim director of the Office of Research and Evaluation Studies, Antioch College, Yellow Springs, Ohio. She is also executive editor of the Journal on Excellence in College Teaching and director of the Lilly Conference on College Teaching–West.

Although the preparation of students to be college teachers is not its primary goal, graduate school is the gateway through which all academics must pass. The growth of Ph.D. programs after World War II has shaped the nature of the academy and the professoriate.

Graduate Education and the U.S. Faculty

Laurie Richlin

American higher education developed as a pocket industry, growing in response to specific markets as they occurred. By the early nineteenth century, higher education was marked most of all by its diversity in types of institutions, in departmental cultures, and in faculty lives. Today, there remain significant differences among types of institutions in how faculty spend their time, how they collaborate with one another and relate to students, and how their research is funded. Yet, in one significant way, colleges and universities of different types are similar. They cultivate an ethos that emulates the research university.

Centripetal Force on Higher Education

This change from highly differentiated institutions to greater similarity among them came about through an "academic revolution," the professionalization of faculty that turned the community of scholars from their local rewards within their institutions to the cosmopolitan "invisible colleges" of their disciplines (Jencks and Riesman, 1977). It is this close tie between research and the university that distinguishes higher education institutions in the United States from their European counterparts. The U.S. university is a knowledge factory.

Where, prior to World War II, a faculty member would have been identified only as part of the profession of university teaching, by the mid-1960s the professionalization of the disciplines made the university connection "incidental" (Nisbet, 1967, p. 19). According to Ladd (1985, p. 157),

New Directions for Teaching and Learning, no. 54, Summer 1993 © Jossey-Bass Publishers

"Whether or not they themselves do research or want to engage in original scholarship, most faculty seem to believe the most meritorious behavior of an academic man or woman is the performance of significant research." Dunham (1969, p. 96) calls this situation "schizophrenic," following "David Reisman's notion of the academic procession, the snakelike movement by which every institution tries to be a Harvard. . . . The blunt fact is that the kind of work that goes on in an academic department within a major university is different from what goes on in the corresponding department even within a fine college with an excellent reputation."

Most schools try to emulate the research universities because there are Ph.D.'s teaching in all segments of American higher education who are "already imbued with the research ethos" from their own graduate training (Bowen and Schuster, 1986, p. 150). The impact of the research university, through its training of Ph.D.'s, began after World War II. As Boyer (1990, p. 10) has observed, "Soon, a veritable army of freshly minted Ph.D.s fanned out to campuses across the country. Inspired by their mentors, this new generation of faculty found themselves committed not only to their institutions but also to their professions. Young scholars sought to replicate the research climate they themselves had experienced. . . . In the new climate, discipline-based departments became the foundation of faculty allegiance, and being a 'scholar' was now virtually synonymous with being an academic professional."

Ph.D.'s take positions at liberal arts colleges only if there are no university positions available (Dent, 1967). Colleges without graduate programs hire Ph.D.'s even though they may fear the impact of those who "may not be happy or complacent at a terminal college, and who may also make others less happy or complacent" (Jencks and Riesman, 1977, p. 25). "A Ph.D. at a state college," states Dunham (1969, p. 164), "will always compare . . . status with a colleague at the state university and will seek to do the same kind of things and want to receive the same kind of rewards." According to Bowen and Schuster (1986, p. 218), "New appointees commonly find themselves at institutions about which they had known little or nothing and which they would have studiously avoided in a more favorable academic market." London (1985, p. 277) has expressed this point even more strongly: "Other than a conscript army, it is difficult to think of a work institution in our society with tens of thousands of frontline employees who have both aspired and trained to work elsewhere."

A Holistic Attempt at Change

The consideration of alternate graduate degrees, particularly those that address more practical aspects of college teaching, is not a new concern. Hollis (1945) acknowledged complaints from employers that the then-current doctoral students had too narrow a focus. He envisioned a wider program that appraised and educated in terms of six factors: teaching, research, personal qualities, standing in the profession, participation in departmental and university planning, and participation in community affairs. Yet, he also worried that a graduate degree for college teachers would attract "hordes of plodding students who are only interested and capable in succeeding in practical programs, more narrowly vocational in nature than those already offered by graduate professional schools on the campus" (1945, pp. 188–189).

Berelson, in his 1957 survey, asked his respondents about their attitudes toward alternate degrees. Their conclusions were emphatic: The master's degree had lost status and would not suffice as the "acceptable degree for college teachers" (Berelson, 1960, p. 228). He found that efforts to "supplant the Ph.D. with an equivalent, but different, doctoral degree have never succeeded" (p. 228). About one-quarter of the graduate faculty that he surveyed thought that the "single [Ph.D.] program is seriously deficient and should be changed," while the rest were split between views that a "single program is best for all" and "the single program may not be best, but it's the only practicable one" (p. 89). When graduate deans were asked the same question in 1990, only 14.2 percent felt that a "single program was seriously deficient," while 43.1 percent considered the "single program best for all," and 42.7 percent thought a single program was "not best but the only practicable one" (Richlin, 1991, p. 132). Berelson (1960, p. 90) warned that a separate program for college teachers that had no dissertation faced three problems: getting "good institutions" to offer the program, getting "good students" to enter them, and getting "good colleges" to hire the graduates. In a survey of graduate deans and program chairs at doctorate-granting institutions regarding their likelihood of offering an alternate doctorate, and of academic deans and department chairs at non-doctorate-granting institutions regarding their likelihood of hiring the graduates, much greater interest was reported in hiring the graduates of those programs than of offering the degrees (Richlin, 1991; see Richlin, this volume, Chapter Ten, for a fuller account of the results of that survey).

One major attempt to answer the complaints about teaching in the universities in the 1960s (in addition to the teaching assistant [TA] training and faculty development movements) came from the Carnegie Corporation, which designed and funded a Doctor of Arts (D.A.) degree to be "less research-oriented than the Ph.D., but more subject-oriented than the Ed.D." (Glazer, 1989, p. 2; see also Gaff and Wilson, 1971). Although D.A. programs continue to exist (see Glazer, this volume), it is generally thought that they "didn't work, while the Ph.D. often works well" (LaPidus, 1987, p. 8), and that disciplines generally would prefer a flexible Ph.D. program allowing for a broader definition of scholarship so as to improve teaching (see, for instance, Jackson, 1990, p. 266). As Boyer (1990, p. 70) has noted, "Some critics [of the Ph.D.] have urged a Doctor of Arts for those interested in college teaching. It's our position that this two-track approach is not desirable. The graduate program should change, not the degree."

Timing of Preparation for an Academic Career

Although there are two points in an academic career when education for college teaching might start—as part of the graduate program or for new faculty hires—there are at least three important reasons why the best time is during the graduate experience. First, there is less ego involvement in personal teaching ability at that time. The introduction of teaching instruction to active faculty has been hampered by the misperception that the "craft of teaching" is not a topic for discussion.

Second, intervention should occur as early as possible in the academic career. The recent study from the Center for Instructional Development at Syracuse University (Diamond and Gray, 1987) reported that among the graduate TAs surveyed across the nation, 75 percent planned to teach in colleges or universities when they completed their degrees (over 50 percent in every field except architecture, communications, and law); in science and mathematics, the figure was 67 percent; in education, 79 percent; and in social sciences, 97 percent.

For a large percentage of faculty, college teaching begins with teaching assistantships. LaPidus (1987, pp. 3–4, 10) noted that "efforts to train people to become teachers are few and are directed primarily toward teaching assistants. These activities usually are discipline based, and are extremely variable in adequacy, intensity, and quality across departments and institutions. . . . The teaching assistants' experience in graduate school forms another part of the process and must be taken seriously as part of the development of faculty members."

The third reason for targeting graduate students for learning about teaching is the impact that their abilities have on undergraduate education. In fact, the first recommendation made by the Study Group on the Conditions of Excellence in American Higher Education (1985, p. 15) is that "college administrators should reallocate faculty and other institutional resources toward increased service to first- and second-year undergraduates." The study group stated as a corollary to its recommendation that "department chairs in institutions employing graduate students as instructors should use them selectively and take measures to ensure that they are well prepared for their responsibilities" (p. 25).

Graduate students teach a significant proportion of lower-level courses at major research institutions. For instance, at the University of California, Berkeley and Davis campuses, TAs teach about 30 percent of the undergraduate classes (McMillen, 1986; State of California, 1987). Another study showed that 45 percent of classes and recitation groups in leading mathematics departments are taught by TAs or part-timers (McMillen, 1986).

Richlin (1987) surveyed the largest (in terms of number of doctorates awarded) graduate departments of chemistry, psychology, and education in the United States and found that ninety-one of ninety-seven departments used doctoral students as teachers of undergraduates, and over half of the TAs taught more than fifty students (pp. 9–10).

Although the best time for beginning preparation for college teaching is during the graduate program, Sell (1987) found that graduate schools do not see themselves as responsible for preparing future faculty. In fact, LaPidus (1987) and Schuster (1987, this volume) challenge graduate schools to take that responsibility.

As Ronkowski (this volume) discusses, there is much to consider in how graduate students develop their synoptic capacity, pedagogical content knowledge, and knowledge of meaning making on the way to becoming scholarly teachers. The effort to refocus graduate education to include preparation of future college teachers will require an understanding by graduate faculty of the developmental stages of pedagogical scholarship.

Socialization of Graduate Students: The Need for Diversity

Doctoral students modify their self-concepts through contact with others. Joseph Katz called mother and graduate school the strongest influences on academics (Schuster, 1990, p. 68). Schuster (1990, p. 73) observed that "there is much more to becoming a professor than simply becoming a competent anthropologist, engineer, historian, micro-biologist," and that the "apprentice phase" of graduate school is the "most enduring" influence on that process (p. 68). For Mark Ingraham, graduate school is a gateway into the "community of scholars," a process that produces a "loyalty to the subject rather than loyalty to learning" (American Association of University Professors Panel, 1960, p. 297; see also Koerin, 1980). Unfortunately, as Hauerwas (1988, p. 26) pointed out, "A Ph.D. too often is the way that we make sure that our knowledge of the past is appropriately fossilized in living representatives who continue to underwrite the knowledge by passing it on through the contemporary university."

Bess (1978) surveyed 236 pre-graduate students intending to attend one university and compared the characteristics of the 87 who aspired to be faculty with a faculty group. The results showed that the aspirants and faculty were so similar that graduate school was not needed to socialize the newcomers. The students anticipated the "values and orientations which [would] be required of them as faculty members," and as undergraduates they "drift[ed] into the academic profession on the basis of inadequate and often misleading information" (1978, p. 312). Because "grades and achievements in the cognitive domain tend to be emphasized, . . . evocative teaching skills are downplayed or missed" (p. 312), and graduate students are the undergraduate students who succeed in this academic narrowing process (p. 296).

The Dissertation

As Berelson (1960, p. 12) noted, the "demands of research and training for research, culminating in the doctoral dissertation, have been at the heart of controversies about graduate study from the start." "Near the center of many issues in doctoral study—its purpose, program, quality, and duration—stands the doctoral dissertation," Berelson wrote. "Sooner or later the debate gets to it, and any decisions about it are likely to affect most other areas of graduate education" (p. 172). In his 1957 survey, Berelson asked his respondents about the purpose, length, and type of research and the role of the dissertation director in the dissertation process. Fifteen percent of graduate faculty thought that the "value of the dissertation is primarily as an original contribution to knowledge," and 57 percent thought of it "primarily as an exercise in research training" (1960, p. 174).

Carmichael (1961, p. 148) found "no consensus among graduate faculties as to [the dissertation's] purpose, its optimum length, the amount of supervision its writer should have, or the nature of the topic that should be chosen." The Council of Graduate Schools (1982, p. 9) listed two purposes for the dissertation in its policy statement: (1) an intensive, highly professional activity that shows a candidate can "carry out and report on scholarly research at the high level of professional competence" and (2) results that "constitute a contribution to knowledge in the field." Bledstein (1976, p. 94) noted that "the Ph.D. dissertation was an exercise not only in scholarly method, but in human endurance and delayed gratification necessary to make an 'original contribution to knowledge.' " Quinton (1980, p. 93) called the "original contribution to knowledge" of the dissertation a "crucial element" of the Ph.D.

Passmore (1980, p. 52) asked whether a graduate student can "master a subject to the degree to which a college educator needs to have mastered it, without embarking on a reasonably large-scale piece of research" and quoted from the 1954 report of the Committee of Fifteen: "We believe that the dissertation can, and should be, one of the most exciting intellectual experiences of the future college teacher. It should be primarily a contribution to the knowledge of its author, an instrument of his intellectual growth, and the result of an adventure, not necessarily into virgin territory, but into the world of ideas that are worth wrestling with." In the humanities, Passmore added, students "don't wrestle with unfamiliar territory, but tackle a familiar problem to see if they can cope with it" (p. 53). They work on the "limited pieces of a puzzle" that are next on the professor's research agenda (p. 54). Current criticism of the dissertation is typified by Sykes's (1988, pp. 15–16) diatribe: "The doctoral dissertation was the perfect vehicle for the shaping of this new breed of professor. Instead of insisting that would-be professors extend the range and breadth of their learning, the new academy insisted the Ph.D. candidate choose a subject of exquisite narrowness and produce 100 or 200 pages of detailed research. . . . Where doing research had once been considered valuable because it helped a professor teach a subject better, research was now an end in itself."

Beginning in August 1989, a committee of the Council of Graduate Schools, composed of graduate school deans, began looking at the role and nature of the doctoral dissertation (Council of Graduate Schools, 1991; Hamilton, this volume). They found wide variation in the range of thought, opinions, and options regarding doctoral research and the dissertation, particularly across different types of disciplines. For instance, in the natural sciences there was more tolerance for dissertations based on previously published work and dissertations written by multiple authors than was found in the humanities or social sciences. The committee's definitions of originality, significance, and independence serve to illustrate the variety of conceptions and approaches that characterize doctoral study.

Learning to Teach

King (1967, p. 96) said that while it did not bother him that graduate schools have no programs to prepare college teachers, he did not like the fact that graduate students are "indoctrinated against undergraduate education." Katz (1976, p. 118) reported that "socialization in graduate school does more than just neglect teaching, it conditions students to belittle it." Many students begin by wanting to teach but "have it socialized out of them" in a society where becoming anything but a researcher is failure (Katz and Hartnett, 1976, p. 273). In mathematics, for example, graduate training, according to Stephen Rodi, "promotes a culture which is antagonistic to undergraduate instruction" because the competitive nature of mathematics graduate education makes the "future teacher both unreceptive toward and unskilled in the techniques of cooperative learning" (Jackson, 1990, p. 267). This sentiment is echoed by Ronald Douglas, who called the first years in graduate school a "Darwinian struggle" (Jackson, 1990, p. 268), and by D. J. Lewis, who labeled the qualifying examination a "hazing ritual" (Jackson, 1990, p. 267). Merriam (1986, p. 108) has expressed much the same opinion: "Worse still, the graduate research training programs, from which most university professors come, too often develop contempt for undergraduate teaching."

Hauerwas (1988, p. 23) has called graduate school "an extended initiation into a guild through which one is taught to think the way the masters of that guild would have us think." He reported that "the realization that my vocation in life was to teach . . . came as a bit of a surprise to me for during my graduate work . . . it never occurred to me that I was training to be a teacher. . . . Nothing in graduate school had prepared me for my beginning awareness that most of my life would be consumed by the effort to learn to teach" (p. 21). Even years later, when he was asked to write an essay to "enculturate" graduate students interested in becoming college teachers, he observed that "being asked to write a manual on how to be an academic . . . seems analogous to being asked to write a sex manual. What has happened that we now do not seem to know how to do what everyone thought was a matter of nature and/or a fairly simple learning procedure?" (p. 19).

The disparity between graduate school preparation and the need for faculty to be able to teach to earn a living has been addressed by graduate programs, if at all, on a piecemeal basis. A 1949 conference on graduate education concluded that "the American college teacher is the only high level professional man in the American scene who enters upon a career with neither the prerequisite trial of competence nor experience in the use of the tools of his profession" (Wise, 1967, p. 77). According to Fraher (1984, pp. 116–117),

> Professors are trained only as scholars and then thrust in front of the classroom to play the role of teacher. . . . The assumption that knowledge of a subject implies the ability to teach in that field permeates American higher education, and one result is that our colleagues generally believe that the problems associated with teaching should disappear as the competent scholar eases past the initial nervousness. . . . It is probably important for most of us to concede that we were not well trained as teachers while we were being prepared as scholars. . . . It is less important in most cases for a teacher to perform impressively as a scholar than it is to facilitate the learning of students.

As Boehrer and Sarkisian (1985, p. 15) put it, "Unlike doctors and many other professionals, most college teachers practice on their clients without benefit of formal training."

Teaching as an Intellectual Activity

According to Cross (1990a, 1990b), to be considered scholarly, teaching must be understood as an intellectual activity. Arrowsmith (1967, pp. 57, 60) noted that "so long as the teacher is viewed as merely a diffuser of knowledge or a higher popularizer, his position will necessarily be a modest and even menial one. . . . For if the teacher stands to the scholar as the pianist to the composer, there can be no question of parity. . . . Our entire educational enterprise is in fact founded upon the wholly false premise that *at some prior stage* the essential educational work has been done." Arrowsmith advocated the "divorcing" of research and teaching, "since the only likely alternative is to make teaching the lackey of scholarship" (p. 71).

Hauerwas (1988, pp. 23–24) has made "a more substantive claim about the importance of teaching for sustaining intellectual growth. Teaching is not just the way we get paid in order to sustain our research, but our most important intellectual resource to challenge the current captivity of the university to the 'disciplines.' . . . When teaching becomes solely a matter of expertise, the very nature of scholarship is perverted or our specialization or discipline legitimates what might be inconvenient to know." Fitzgerald (1989, p. 3) contends that "teaching is a vocation or occupation which requires both intellectual skills and advanced training. Hence, by this definition teaching is composed of two distinct parts: mastery of a specific body of knowledge plus advanced training in the dissemination and application of this knowledge in the professional area."

In searching for the precollegiate "expert pedagogue," Berliner (1986, p. 13) found change and growth in abilities between novice and expert teachers:

> We sometimes seem to have problems with our perception of teachers' skillfulness, categorizing it as mere practice. We often confuse the cognition necessary for exemplary performance with the validity of the course of action. When an expert physics problem solver takes time and announces that the problem involves Newton's second law, he or she is an expert. When an experienced teacher takes time and classifies a child's learning problems into three categories that lead to a particular set of actions, it is often considered to be an example of something less. We make a great mistake if we confuse the validity of the inferences with the inference making process. . . . Practical problem solving, it seems, has a kind of low-class reputation. Because the sources of professional knowledge for a teacher are highly bound by time, materials, and place, we call it practical knowledge. But it now appears that such domain-specific knowledge is a characteristic of every kind of expert. In other fields we honor such knowledge. In education, it is merely practical, and what is often implied is that such knowledge is less complex, less understandable, or less amenable to scientific study.

Ronkowski (this volume) describes the developmental growth from novice to expert by beginning college teachers and differentiates between learning to teach as a *bricoleur* ("do-it-yourselfer") versus as an intellectual activity (also see Ronkowski, 1989). For Shulman (1990) "Teaching will be considered a scholarly activity only when professors develop a conception of pedagogy that is very tightly coupled to scholarship in the disciplines themselves." "The conception of pedagogical reasoning places emphasis upon the intellectual basis for teaching performance rather than on behavior alone" (Shulman, 1987, p. 20). It is the "integral relationships between teaching and the scholarly domains of the liberal arts" (p. 20) that Shulman believes should inform the education of future teachers. He sees three necessities for creating the new type of scholar: a community designed to stimulate discourse around pedagogical scholarship; a conception of scholarship that reconnects it to teaching, deeply rooted in the disciplines that comprise the rest of academic scholarship; and mechanisms for bringing the scholarship and community together (Shulman, 1990). He believes that it is necessary to start with the discipline, not the technique, to improve teaching. Even the approaches to teaching (for example, collaborative versus individual) differ by subject area (Roskens, 1983).

James Conant observed that a "field could be called scientific when knowledge has accumulated, progress is evident in the development of new conceptual schemes resulting from experiments and observations, and conceptual schemes lead, in turn, to more research" (McKeachie, 1990, p. 189). McKeachie (1990, p. 189) looked at the field of pedagogy and found that it "clearly meets Conant's criteria for a scientific field." With what has been discovered already about learning, he noted that the "frontier of knowledge about college teaching thus becomes even more challenging" (p. 197).

Summary

Since World War II, preparation of the American faculty has moved toward professionalization within the disciplines, facilitated by the narrow research focus of graduate education. However, as research-trained Ph.D.'s have entered the professoriate, they have found that their main occupation is teaching undergraduates, for which they are unprepared. This volume explores several aspects of graduate education relating to the preparation of future college professors for a broader conception of scholarship, including analysis of past attempts to design graduate programs to better prepare college teachers, the responsibility of graduate schools for training the faculty of the future, the need to include diverse voices in the academy, and specific recommendations for incorporating new forms of disciplinary integration, professional practice, and pedagogical scholarship into graduate programs.

References

American Association of University Professors Panel. "Graduate Training for College Teaching: A Panel Discussion." *AAUP Bulletin,* 1960, *46,* 294–299.

Arrowsmith, W. "The Future of Teaching." In C.B.T. Lee (ed.), *Improving College Teaching.* Washington, D.C.: American Council on Education, 1967.

Berelson, B. *Graduate Education in the United States.* New York: McGraw-Hill, 1960.

Berliner, D. C. "In Pursuit of the Expert Pedagogue." *Educational Researcher,* 1986, *15* (7), 5–13.

Bess, J. L. "Anticipatory Socialization of Graduate Students." *Research in Higher Education,* 1978, *8* (4), 289–317.

Bledstein, B. *The Culture of Professionalism: The Middle Class and the Development of Higher Education in America.* New York: Norton, 1976.

Boehrer, J., and Sarkisian, E. "The Teaching Assistant's Point of View." In J.D.W. Andrews (ed.), *Strengthening the Teaching Assistant Faculty.* New Directions for Teaching and Learning, no. 22. San Francisco: Jossey-Bass, 1985.

Bowen, H. R., and Schuster, J. H. *American Professors: A National Resource Imperiled.* New York: Oxford University Press, 1986.

Boyer, E. L. *Scholarship Reconsidered: Priorities of the Professoriate.* Princeton, N.J.: Princeton University Press, 1990.

Carmichael, D. C. *Graduate Education: A Critique and a Program.* New York: HarperCollins, 1961.

Council of Graduate Schools. *The Doctor of Philosophy Degree: A Policy Statement.* Washington, D.C.: Council of Graduate Schools, 1982.

Council of Graduate Schools. *The Role and Nature of the Doctoral Dissertation.* Washington, D.C.: Council of Graduate Schools, 1991.

Cross, K. P. "The New American Scholar: The Scholarship of Teaching." Address presented at the Scholarship of Teaching conference, Iona College, New Rochelle, New York, October 1990a.

Cross, K. P. "Teachers as Scholars." *AAHE Bulletin,* 1990b, *43,* 3–5.

Dent, A. W. "Effects of Teacher Shortage on Small Undergraduate Colleges." In C.B.T. Lee (ed.), *Improving College Teaching.* Washington, D.C.: American Council on Education, 1967.

Diamond, R. M., and Gray, P. *National Study of Teaching Assistants.* Syracuse, N.Y.: Center for Instructional Development, Syracuse University, 1987.

Dunham, E. A. *Colleges of the Forgotten Americans: A Profile of State Colleges and Regional Universities.* New York: McGraw-Hill, 1969.

Fitzgerald, R. G. "The Teaching Doctorate: A Need for Teaching Credentials in Higher Education." *The PEN,* September–October 1989, pp. 3–5.

Fraher, R. "Learning a New Art: Suggestions for Beginning Teachers." In M. M. Gullette (ed.), *The Art and Craft of Teaching.* Cambridge, Mass.: Harvard University Press, 1984.

Gaff, J. G., and Wilson, R. C. "The Teaching Environment." *AAUP Bulletin,* 1971, *57,* 475–493.

Glazer, J. S. "The Fate of the Doctorate of Arts Degree." Paper presented at the annual meeting of the Association for the Study of Higher Education, Atlanta, November 1989.

Hauerwas, S. M. "The Morality of Teaching." In A. L. DeNeef, C. D. Goodwin, and E. S. McCrate (eds.), *The Academic's Handbook.* Durham, N.C.: Duke University Press, 1988.

Hollis, E. V. *Toward Improving Ph.D. Programs.* Washington, D.C.: American Council on Education, 1945.

Jackson, A. "Graduate Education in Mathematics: Is It Working?" *Notices of the American Mathematical Society,* 1990, *37,* 266–268.

Jencks, C., and Riesman, D. *The Academic Revolution.* (2nd ed.) Chicago: University of Chicago Press, 1977.

Katz, J. "Development of the Mind." In J. Katz and R. T. Hartnett (eds.), *Scholars in the Making.* New York: Ballinger, 1976.

Katz, J., and Hartnett, R. T. "Recommendations for Training Better Scholars." In J. Katz and R. T. Hartnett (eds.), *Scholars in the Making.* New York: Ballinger, 1976.

King, J. E. "The Need for In-Service Programs." In C.B.T. Lee (ed.), *Improving College Teaching.* Washington, D.C.: American Council on Education, 1967.

Koerin, B. B. "Teaching Effectiveness and Faculty Development Programs: A Review." *Journal of General Education,* 1980, *32,* 40–51.

Ladd, E. C., Jr. "The Work Experience of American Professors: Some Data and an Argument." In M. J. Finkelstein (ed.), *ASHE Reader on Faculty and Faculty Issues in Colleges and Universities.* Lexington, Mass.: Ginn Press, 1985.

LaPidus, J. B. "The Role of Graduate Education in the Preparation of Faculty." Paper presented at the annual National Conference on Higher Education, American Association for Higher Education, Chicago, March 1987.

London, H. B. "The Community College Teacher." In M. J. Finkelstein (ed.), *ASHE Reader on Faculty and Faculty Issues in Colleges and Universities.* Lexington, Mass.: Ginn Press, 1985.

McKeachie, W. J. "Research on College Teaching: The Historical Background." *Journal of Educational Psychology*, 1990, *82* (2), 189–200.

McMillen, L. "Teaching Assistants Get Increased Training: Problems Arise in Foreign-Student Programs." *Chronicle of Higher Education*, October 29, 1986, p. 18.

Merriam, R. W. "Academic Research vs. the Liberal Arts." *Journal of College Science Teaching*, 1986, *16*, 105–109.

Nisbet, R. A. "Conflicting Academic Loyalties." In C.B.T. Lee (ed.), *Improving College Teaching*. Washington, D.C.: American Council on Education, 1967.

Passmore, J. "The Philosophy of Graduate Education." In W. K. Frankena (ed.), *The Philosophy and Future of Graduate Education*. Ann Arbor: University of Michigan Press, 1980.

Quinton, A. "Reflections on the Graduate School." In W. K. Frankena (ed.), *The Philosophy and Future of Graduate Education*. Ann Arbor: University of Michigan Press, 1980.

Richlin, L. "Survey of Largest TA Programs." Unpublished manuscript, Claremont Graduate School, 1987.

Richlin, L. "Preparing Future Faculty: Meeting the Need for Teacher-Scholars by Enlarging the View of Scholarship in Ph.D. Programs." Unpublished doctoral dissertation, Department of Education, Claremont Graduate School, 1991.

Ronkowski, S. "Changes in Teaching Assistant Concerns Over Time." Paper presented at the 2nd national conference on the Training and Employment of Teaching Assistants, Seattle, November 1989. (ERIC HE 023 178; ED 315 012; RIE, June 1990)

Roskens, R. W. "Implications of Biglan Model Research for the Process of Faculty Advancement." *Research in Higher Education*, 1983, *18* (3), 285–297.

Schuster, J. H. "Preparation of the American Professor: A Graduate School Responsibility." Paper presented at the 43rd annual meeting of the Midwestern Association of Graduate Schools, Chicago, April 1987.

Schuster, J. H. "Strengthening Career Preparation for Prospective Professors." In J. H. Schuster, D. W. Wheeler, and Associates, *Enhancing Faculty Careers: Strategies for Development and Renewal*. San Francisco: Jossey-Bass, 1990.

Sell, G. R. "Preparing Teaching Assistants as Future Faculty: Is This Really the University's Objective?" Paper presented at the annual meeting of the Association for the Study of Higher Education, Baltimore, November 1987.

Shulman, L. S. "Knowledge and Teaching: Foundations of the New Reform." *Harvard Educational Review*, 1987, *57*, 1–22.

Shulman, L. S. "The New American Scholar: A Teacher of Substance." Address presented at the Scholarship of Teaching conference, Iona College, New Rochelle, New York, October 1990.

State of California. *Resolution Chapter 102 of Assembly Concurrent Resolution No. 39*. Sacramento: State of California, 1987.

Study Group on the Conditions of Excellence in American Higher Education. National Institute of Education. *Involvement in Learning: Realizing the Potential of American Higher Education*. Washington, D.C.: Government Printing Office, 1985.

Sykes, C. J. *Profscam: Professors and the Demise of Higher Education*. Washington, D.C.: Regnery Gateway, 1988.

Wise, W. M. "Who Teaches the Teachers?" In C.B.T. Lee (ed.), *Improving College Teaching*. Washington, D.C.: American Council on Education, 1967.

LAURIE RICHLIN is interim director of the Office of Research and Evaluation Studies, Antioch College, Yellow Springs, Ohio. She is also executive editor of the Journal on Excellence in College Teaching *and director of the Lilly Conference on College Teaching–West.*

The development and current status of the Doctor of Arts, an innovative degree designed to prepare college teachers, are analyzed, and several conclusions are drawn regarding the efficacy and acceptability of a teaching doctorate.

The Doctor of Arts: Retrospect and Prospect

Judith S. Glazer

The advent of the Doctor of Arts (D.A.) occurred during the 1960s, a decade of unprecedented expansion in higher education, and in the context of great social turmoil. Its rationale derived from criticism analogous to that expressed today, namely, Ph.D. programs are overly concerned with specialized research and undergraduate teaching is being neglected at a time when the community college sector, in particular, is rapidly expanding.

The D.A. originated at Carnegie-Mellon University in conjunction with the establishment of an education center for teacher training and curriculum reform. It was perceived as a major innovation that could reform the doctorate by changing its focus from the development of research scholars to the preparation of college teachers. It gained generous financial support from the Carnegie Corporation (Dunham, 1969) and vigorous endorsements from the Carnegie Commission on Higher Education (1971, 1972) under the leadership of Clark Kerr, who predicted that it would become "the standard degree for college teaching in the United States, a non-research degree of high prestige" (1970, p. vii). The D.A. was subsequently sanc-

This study has been completed with assistance from TIAA-CREF and the C. W. Post Campus Research Fund. I thank Peggy Lane for her assistance in the development and analysis of a national survey of D.A. recipients. Thanks are also extended to Estela Bensimon and Yvonna Lincoln for their helpful comments on earlier drafts and to Lori Charnow and the staff of the Doctorate Records Project. I am deeply indebted to the deans, faculty, and graduates who took the time to respond to my questions and who provided me with important insights into their D.A. programs.

tioned by three professional associations, the Council of Graduate Schools (1970a, 1970b), the American Association of State Colleges and Universities (Committee on Graduate Studies, 1970), and the National Association of Community and Junior Colleges (1969), each of which promulgated guidelines for its development and support within member institutions. It was embraced by state policy boards in New York, Tennessee, Illinois, Michigan, Idaho, and Washington that were seeking ways to discourage the expansion of Ph.D. programs and to foster faculty development in the community college sector. Between 1967 and 1976, the Carnegie Corporation provided twenty-one public and private universities and the New York State Board of Regents with $3.2 million in planning grants and fellowship support to design and implement one or more D.A. programs in liberal arts and professional fields. At its peak, the D.A. was offered in twenty-seven departments and thirty-five fields at thirty-two universities, almost equally divided between research and doctorate-granting institutions.

Development of D.A. Models

The D.A. was originally endorsed in preference to the Ed.D. for liberal arts majors as a professional degree combining disciplinary specialization, the study of related disciplines, professional preparation in a teaching field, one or more internships, and a scholarly research project (Dressel and DeLisle, 1972). In 1974, a second, more interdisciplinary model was advanced as a means of making the D.A. more distinctive and with the objective of producing generalists who could demonstrate broad knowledge in more than one teaching field (Dressel and Thompson, 1974). As the D.A. became more professionalized, a third model evolved to provide advanced preparation for experienced practitioners in government, business and industry, and nonprofit organizations. In New York, Tennessee, and Virginia, the decision to professionalize the D.A. was a pragmatic response by universities to the demands of legislatures and state governing boards that new doctoral programs be sufficiently distinctive and not duplicate existing Ph.D. and Ed.D. programs. Examples of such special-purpose D.A.'s are those in humanistic studies at the State University of New York in Albany, communicative disorders at Adelphi University, physical education at Middle Tennessee State University, and community college education at George Mason University. Most programs, regardless of the model, incorporate six basic components: (1) twenty-four to thirty-six credits of coursework in the major field, (2) twelve to eighteen credits in one or more cognate fields, (3) nine to eighteen credits in professional skills, (4) one to four internships or externships, (5) written or oral comprehensive qualifying examinations, or both, and (6) a research project or dissertation and an oral defense.

    Admission Criteria. To recruit students with demonstrated competence in teaching fields, D.A. programs tend to give less emphasis to

Graduate Record Examination scores, foreign language proficiency, and research skills. Criteria for admission stress evidence of teaching experience, commitment to teaching undergraduates, and, in the case of such nonteaching fields as library management, appropriate academic and professional credentials. In the first decade of operation, Carnegie grants were designated specifically for fellowship support of D.A. candidates, accelerating the time to completion of the degree to 3 years of full-time attendance. Once these funds were exhausted in the mid-1970s, the competition for scarce resources to support doctoral students intensified, and admission criteria were modified to permit part-time attendance, increasing the median registered time-to-degree to 7.8 years in 1989–1991 (Doctorate Records Project, 1991).

Coursework. Course requirements of the D.A. presume that effective teaching in a discipline derives from breadth of knowledge combined with the ability to convey that knowledge to undergraduates. Programs typically require candidates to complete concentrations in two or three teaching fields, at least one of which must be outside the declared major. For example, the economics major at Illinois State University has sixteen options, including higher education economics, business, marketing, organizational behavior, political science, and public policy. A cluster of education courses, generally offered within the arts and science framework rather than through colleges of education, is designed to increase competence in course development, teaching methods, instructional technology, and student evaluation. At the University of Illinois in Chicago, D.A. candidates in chemistry, biology, and mathematics complete an integrated cluster of courses in instructional design and technology, computer instruction, research in education settings, laboratory teaching methods, and psychological foundations of postsecondary education.

Internship and Practicum. The internship is perceived as the component that most clearly distinguishes the D.A. from the Ph.D. However, from the outset, the high rate of variability in what should constitute the internship and the criteria for its inclusion have been identified as an inherent weakness of D.A. programs (Dressel and Thompson, 1974). The most common approach, which in many ways resembles the traditional teaching assistantship, engages the student in one or more semesters of teaching undergraduates under the supervision of departmental faculty. A more innovative approach has been the incorporation of a sequence of instructional design and evaluation experiences that introduce students to models of teaching and learning, assessment techniques, and externships at nearby community colleges. Since many students enroll with teaching experience, the internship is frequently waived, as I found in a recent survey of 350 graduates, 19 percent of whom noted that they had received waivers (Glazer, 1992).

Final Project. The D.A. differs most dramatically from the Ph.D. in its deemphasis of the traditional research dissertation. Although some programs retain a traditional dissertation, this is not the general practice. New York State guidelines specify that the final project must be a research essay. Program directors employ such descriptors as interpretive, analytical, expository, creative, and scholarly in describing their dissertation requirements. D.A. graduates who responded to my survey variously categorized their final projects as a dissertation (32 percent), curriculum thesis (25 percent), research essay (17 percent), treatise (16 percent), educational project (6 percent), or creative work (4 percent) (Glazer, 1992). A review of 1,189 dissertation abstracts found 41 percent with some reference to teaching in the title and another 6 percent involving such creative projects as novels, poetry, musical compositions, and works of art (Gingerich, 1991).

Currently Known Status of D.A. Programs

A total of 1,762 D.A. degrees were awarded between 1967 and 1990. For 1990, the Doctorate Records Project (1991) reported data on 36,057 doctorates. The D.A. accounted for 100 (.3 percent) of this total compared to the Ph.D. and D.S.C. (87.4 percent), Ed.D. (9.4 percent) and all other doctorates (2.9 percent). The humanities accounted for 59 percent of all earned D.A.'s, whereas the physical sciences and life sciences accounted for 17.4 percent, education for 12 percent, and professional fields including engineering for 4.1 percent. A demographic profile of D.A. recipients indicated that 91.4 percent were white, 5 percent black, 2 percent Hispanic, and 1 percent Asian; foreign students accounted for only 9 percent of the total.

Twenty institutions still offer the D.A. (see Table 2.1), and while this figure represents a decline of 39 percent in program offerings over the past two decades (see Table 2.2), the D.A. has found a comfortable niche in the universities that continue to support it. Fifteen of these institutions offer the degree in more than one field of study. The most frequently offered majors are English (nine), history (five), mathematics (five), and chemistry (four). Eight programs are interdisciplinary, among them African American studies, humanistic studies, international studies, Teaching English as a Second Language, and education. The D.A. differs from the Ph.D. in its emphasis on practice, breadth of knowledge, and applied research. It differs from the Ed.D. in the central role given to liberal arts content courses combined with pedagogy. As programs have evolved, they have been modified to reflect institutional mission, state criteria for accreditation, and new disciplinary directions. This evolution has led to new concentrations in rhetoric, linguistics, ecology, and applied history.

Degree Discontinuance. Since 1970, as shown in Table 2.2, fifteen institutions have discontinued the D.A. in all fields; four others have dropped a total of thirteen majors, maintaining only one area based on the

Table 2.1. D.A.-Granting Institutions
and Programs as of Spring 1990

Institution	Program	Degrees
Adelphi University	Communicative Disorders	8
	Mathematics	0
Ball State University	Music	80
	Education	4[a]
Clark-Atlanta University	Education	6[a]
	English	5
	History	0
	Romance Languages	6
	Science Education	3
George Mason University	Community College Education	1
	Education (D.A.Ed.)	25
Idaho State University	Biology	52
	Education	2[a]
	English	48
	Other Humanities	5
	Mathematics	40
	Political Science	36
Illinois State University	Economics	6
	Education	8[a]
	English	31
	History	29
	Mathematics	11
Lehigh University	Chemistry	5
Middle Tennessee State University	Chemistry	2
	Economics	3
	English	40
	History	30
	Physical Education	108
New York University	Art Education	[18[b]]
	Arts Therapy	
	Arts Administration	
	Arts and Humanities	
	Dance and Dance Education	
	Music and Music Education	
	Music Performance and Composition	
	Music Therapy	
	Studio Art	
Simmons College	Library Administration	48
Saint John's University	English	15
	Modern World History	2
	Education	1[a]
State University of New York at Albany	English	65
	Humanistic Studies	20
State University of New York at Stony Brook	Foreign Language Instruction: French, Italian, German, Russian, Spanish	19
	TESOL	7

Table 2.1. (*continued*)

Institution	Program	Degrees
Syracuse University	Foreign Language and Literature	10
University of Illinois at Chicago	Biology	3
	Chemistry	4
	Mathematics	8
	Education	3[a]
University of Miami	Civil Engineering	5
	English	4
	History	12
	Interamerican Studies	9
	International Affairs	5
	Mathematics	10
	Mechanical Engineering	8
University of Michigan	English	108
University of Mississippi	Chemistry	6
	English	11
	Music	26
	Education	6[a]
University of Northern Colorado	Music	69
University of North Dakota	Biology	9
	History	29

Note: TESOL = Teaching English as a Second Language.

[a] The use of education as a field is derived from Doctorate Records Project (1991) data; in some cases it may refer to a degree in education in a liberal arts content area.

[b] Breakdown of the number of degrees conferred per program was not available.

Source: Doctorate Records Project, 1991.

continued commitment of a program director or department chair. The reasons for dropping the D.A. vary considerably and reflect, to some extent, the changes in Carnegie classification status of at least eleven of these institutions from Comprehensive Doctorate Granting to Research 1 and 2 (see Carnegie Foundation for the Advancement of Teaching, 1987, for an explanation of the categorization scheme). Three of the original Carnegie Corporation grantees declined at the time to offer the degree and returned their planning grants. Two of these, Dartmouth College and Massachusetts Institute of Technology, decided that they could reshape their Ph.D. programs to meet the D.A. objectives of preparation for college teaching; the third, Stephen Austin University, was prohibited from offering the D.A. by the Texas Board of Higher Education, which had declared a state moratorium on new degrees. Six universities discontinued the D.A. between 1976 and 1985—Brown University, Claremont Graduate School, Ohio State University, University of the Pacific, University of Washington, and Washington State University—and they were followed in 1989 by Catholic

Table 2.2. Discontinued D.A. Programs as of Spring 1990

Institution	Program	Year	Degrees
Brown University	Creative Writing	1976	3
Carnegie-Mellon University	Chemistry	NA	1
	Education		14[a]
	English		57
	Fine Arts		18
	History		93
	Mathematics		9
Catholic University	English	1990	19
	Education	1990	4[a]
	History	1990	3
	Medical Technology	1990	14
	Spanish	1990	3
Claremont Graduate School	Biology	1980	1
	Economics		2
	Other Humanities		3
Drake University	English		37
Lehigh University	Business/Economics	1980	NA
	Government	1987	25
	Psychology	1980	4
Nova University	Education (D.A.T.L.)	1989	1
	Information Science (D.A.I.S.)	1990	17
Ohio State University	Slavic	1980	2
	Economics	1981	1
Syracuse University	English	1981	14
University of Miami	Economics	1988	12
	Education	1976	6
	Chemistry	1983	2
	Foreign Languages	1988	5
University of Northern Colorado	Biology	1989	38
	Chemistry	1989	11
	Geography	1989	22
	History	1989	3
	Mathematics	1989	29
	Education	1989	3[a]
University of Oregon	English	1989	92
University of the Pacific	English	1980	12
University of Washington	Chemistry	1985	1
	Germanics	1985	9
	Physics	1985	1
Washington State University	Chemistry	1979	1
	Mathematics	1980	1
Western Colorado University	Humanities	1984	NA
	Social Science	1984	NA

Note: NA = data not available, D.A.T.L. = Doctor of Arts-Teaching and Learning, D.A.I.S. = Doctor of Arts-Information Science.

[a] The use of education as a field is derived from Doctorate Records Project (1991) data; in some cases it may refer to a degree in education in a liberal arts content area.

Source: Doctorate Records Project, 1991.

University, University of Northern Colorado, and University of Oregon. The D.A. also became a casualty of an institutional closure when Western Colorado University, established in 1971 as a nonresidential institution, was denied accreditation by the North Central States Association and discontinued operations entirely in 1984. At Carnegie-Mellon, the D.A. is dormant in mathematics and has been discontinued in four other fields due to lack of administrative support. An analogous situation exists at Lehigh University, where chemistry remains the only department with a D.A. option. At Washington State University, the Department of Mathematics recently approved a Ph.D. in mathematics with a teaching emphasis (Ph.D./T.E.) as a teaching doctorate for mathematics majors who otherwise meet all criteria for a research degree. In three other universities, applications are now pending at the state level for conversion of at least one of their D.A. programs to discipline-based Ph.D.'s with teaching emphases. At the University of Michigan, the D.A. in English is offered for community college teachers, the Ed.D. in English education for secondary school teachers, and the Ph.D. in English language and literature as "the basic credential for college faculty." The D.A., in this case, combines coursework in rhetoric, composition theory, literacy, and discourse analysis with a community college internship and a dissertation in the theory and practice of teaching college English.

My interviews with program directors revealed that the decision to discontinue the D.A. resulted from a lack of departmental support, dissatisfaction with the quality of student work, changes in the academic labor market, and a withdrawal of external funding for fellowships. In some cases, program directors noted that termination resulted from a recommendation of independent faculty review committees, central administration, or state coordinating boards. As one director observed, "The D.A. was a noble experiment at the wrong time and perhaps the wrong institution. Its need in English had become less justifiable by the time we introduced it with fewer teaching opportunities in the two-year colleges. We did not have enough human and material resources to support a really strong program and here, at least, we tended to attract people who couldn't manage a research Ph.D. and that hardly seemed a worthy purpose" (Glazer, 1992).

Employment Status of Graduates. One measure of program success is the impact of the degree on its graduates in terms of employment status and participant satisfaction. Respondents to my survey of 350 graduates, conducted in spring 1991 (Glazer, 1992), indicated that students who choose the D.A. opt for a program that will increase their pedagogical content knowledge, make fewer research demands than the Ph.D., enhance their marketability, and fulfill the promise of an innovative approach to the doctorate. Demographic data provided by the survey respondents underscored the in-service nature of the degree; only 16 percent were full-time students when they entered their programs, while 95 percent held master's degrees in the field in which they were obtaining the degree. More than 50 percent changed jobs after graduation, most frequently in education, humanities, and social sciences. Three-fourths of the respondents were teaching, 61 percent in colleges and universities and 15 percent in K–12 school districts. Those who were not teaching described themselves as administrators, consultants, business executives, computer specialists, and staff developers.

Participant Satisfaction. An assumption often made about the doctorate is that programs are comparable across institutions and that, as several individuals in my study indicated in their survey responses, "A doctorate is a doctorate is a doctorate." As a result, one major disappointment of D.A. graduates has been the negative reaction of colleagues toward the D.A. degree. By the same token, several of the respondents viewed their own programs as unique and of a higher quality than others. They implied that the D.A. was not as easy a route as they had assumed at the outset and that their programs were so rigorous, they "could have done a Ph.D. for the same effort." In programs where expectations had not been met or where faculty resistance has been encountered, graduates ascribed these difficulties to the uncertain futures of their particular programs. A feeling of abandonment also was expressed by those whose programs had been terminated in favor of the Ph.D., or where changes in degree designation were being sought.

Conclusions About the Teaching Doctorate

The D.A. has by and large proved useful to its graduates, meeting their goals as practical programs that combine subject matter content and pedagogical skills, and that enable them to secure professional credentials and enhance their teaching careers. However, the impact of the degree has been minimal as an innovation in graduate education. One is hard-pressed to find any reference to the D.A. in either the reform literature on teaching and learning or the literature on the arts and science doctorate.

Schön (1983, p. 26) has argued persuasively that a "model of technical rationality is embedded in the institutional context of professional life [and] is implicit in the institutionalized relations of research and practice, and in the normative curricula of professional education. Even when practitioners, educators, and researchers question the model of technical rationality, they are party to the institutions that perpetuate it." A defining characteristic of the modern university, one that is embedded in the institutional context of academic life, is the research doctorate as signified by the Ph.D. The D.A., on the other hand, represents an alternative model in which practice is elevated to a higher position than research, and, as such, it is incompatible with Schön's model of technical rationality, which so clearly dominates the institutional context of the university.

This incompatibility partially accounts for the lack of receptivity toward the D.A. by graduate faculty and deans intent on protecting the status and prestige of their institutions and using scarce resources to build national reputations as doctorate-granting research institutions. Once the change agents (in this case, the Carnegie Corporation and the state coordinating boards) withdrew their expressed support, and market forces reduced the demand for college teachers, D.A. programs lost academic legitimacy within the education establishment. While D.A. graduates are relatively satisfied with their academic experience, the perceptions of others about the D.A. and the dominance of the research Ph.D. inhibit its growth and threaten its survival. Where the D.A. prospers, it occupies a market niche that is compatible with the institutional culture, one that values and rewards classroom teaching and one in which multidisciplinary and critical approaches to teaching are stressed. In the final analysis, the experiences of those involved in D.A. programs document the continuing dichotomy between individuals who do research and individuals who teach, a dichotomy that remains to be bridged on both the theoretical and practical levels.

References

Carnegie Commission on Higher Education. *Less Time, More Options.* New York: McGraw-Hill, 1971.

Carnegie Commission on Higher Education. *More Effective Use of Resources.* New York: McGraw-Hill, 1972.

Carnegie Foundation for the Advancement of Teaching. *A Classification of Institutions of Higher Education.* Princeton, N.J.: Princeton University Press, 1987.

Committee on Graduate Studies. *The Doctor of Arts Degree: A Proposal for Guidelines.* Washington, D.C.: American Association of State Colleges and Universities, 1970.

Council of Graduate Schools. *The Doctor of Arts Degree.* Washington, D.C.: Council of Graduate Schools, 1970a.

Council of Graduate Schools. *Supplemental Statement on the Doctor of Arts Degree.* Washington, D.C.: Council of Graduate Schools, 1970b.

Doctorate Records Project. *Survey of Earned Doctorates.* Unpublished data, Washington, D.C., 1991.

Dressel, P. L., and DeLisle, F. H. *Blueprint for Change: Doctoral Programs for College Teachers.* Iowa City, Iowa: American College Testing Program, 1972.

Dressel, P. L., and Thompson, M. M. *College Teaching: Improvement by Degrees.* Iowa City, Iowa: American College Testing Program, 1974.

Dunham, E. A. *Colleges of the Forgotten Americans: A Profile of State Colleges and Regional Universities.* New York: McGraw-Hill, 1969.

Gingerich, W. "Doctor of Arts Dissertations/Essays in the University Microfilm International Record: A Report." In B. S. Pulling (ed.), *Proceedings of the D.A. at the Crossroads: A National Conference on the Doctor of Arts Degree.* Pocatello: Idaho State University, 1991.

Glazer, J. S. "The Scholarship of Teaching: The Doctor of Arts Degree." Paper presented at the annual meeting of the American Educational Research Association, San Francisco, April 1992.

Kerr, C. "Preface." In E. A. Dunham, *Colleges for Forgotten Americans: A Profile of State Colleges and Regional Universities.* New York: McGraw-Hill, 1969.

National Association of Community and Junior Colleges. *Guidelines for the Preparation of*

Community/Junior College Teachers. Washington, D.C.: National Faculty Association of Community and Junior Colleges, 1969.

Schön, D. A. *The Reflective Practitioner: How Professionals Think in Action.* New York: Basic Books, 1983.

JUDITH S. GLAZER is associate professor of education in the Department of Curriculum and Instruction at the C. W. Post Campus of Long Island University, Brookville, New York.

With the replacement of over half of the U.S. faculty looming in the proximate future, the task of preparing the next generation of faculty requires a higher priority in graduate education. Graduate schools have the responsibility and the capability to exert greater influence in adequately preparing the new generation of professors.

Preparing the Next Generation of Faculty: The Graduate School's Opportunity

Jack H. Schuster

Among the developments destined to shape higher education in the United States for years to come are two that have far-reaching implications for prioritizing the work of graduate schools. The first is the need to replace scores of thousands of faculty members who will be retiring before the end of the 1990s. The second is the struggle to upgrade the quality of college and university teaching, especially within the venue of undergraduate programs. In each of these pursuits, the American graduate school can play, if it chooses, a more efficacious role than it has in the past. In this chapter, I argue that graduate schools in fact have devoted far too little attention to these two objectives, even though the graduate schools function as the portal through which virtually all prospective professors must pass.

The reality is that American professors universally experience intensive graduate or professional school training. In that process, professors are prepared, socialized, and acculturated during their graduate student years. Jules LaPidus, president of the Council of Graduate Schools, has succinctly expressed this point: "The scholarly nexus through which interested students become faculty members is the graduate schools" (1987, p. 12). As Joseph Katz once suggested, the strongest influence that shapes academics, other than mother, is graduate school, and that tongue-in-cheek claim is probably not much of an exaggeration, if any. However, there is little evidence to suggest that graduate schools, despite their purview of graduate education, normally see the preparation of professors as teaching faculty as one of their more important priorities.

To make the case that graduate schools can and should strive to exert much more influence than they ordinarily do in the preparation of would-be professors, I advance four propositions: (1) The resurgence of interest in enhancing the quality of teaching in postsecondary institutions underscores the need for graduate programs to better prepare future faculty. (2) Graduate schools should play a more prominent role in the preparation of future professors. (3) Graduate schools can, in fact, make a much more substantial contribution in preparing future professors than they typically do. And (4) the outlook for the academic labor market underscores the urgency of an enhanced graduate school role.

Diminution and (Partial) Resuscitation of Teaching

By any reckoning, the attention devoted to teaching in most sectors of American higher education had dwindled during the past two decades. A brief account of how that transpired may be useful. The diminution of teaching was not universal. It did not occur among those colleges—both two- and four-year—whose missions were, and are, focused almost exclusively on teaching undergraduates. Nor did the research focus of the research universities waver during this time. The research universities did not abandon teaching; there previously had not been a large enough commitment to teaching to make desertion (as distinguished from "continuing neglect") a possibility—with due respect for their protests to the contrary. This may be a harsh judgment, but the record at research universities reveals great unevenness in the quality of undergraduate teaching.

Thus, at either end of the institutional teaching-research continuum—those campuses that maintained an essentially pure teaching mission and those that remained ardently committed to research and publication—no change with respect to the importance accorded teaching appears to have occurred. However, a substantial shift toward research at the expense of teaching unquestionably has taken place in many of the hundreds of campuses arrayed between the extremes of that continuum. This shift has been the case especially in the less prestigious doctorate-granting universities, many of which had initiated Ph.D. work during the 1960s boom, in the comprehensive master's-granting institutions, and in the liberal arts colleges, ranging from highly to minimally selective.

Several factors contributed to this reprioritization, but none as much as the dramatic shift in academic labor market conditions that took hold in the early 1970s. At about that time, the supply of prospective faculty, fueled by the legions of Ph.D. earners who were completing their degrees at the growing number of Ph.D.-granting institutions, began to overtake the demand for new faculty. The oversupply in most fields was exacerbated by a downturn in demand due to the recession (some said "new depression") of the early 1970s, which brought an abrupt end to the heady expansion of the previous decade and a half.

A consequence was that hundreds of colleges and universities that previously had not been able to be particularly picky about whom they hired rather suddenly found that they could become considerably more selective. The proportion of new hires who held Ph.D.'s, young faculty members well trained in the skills and culture of research, escalated sharply. Campuses that had not been able realistically to insist that probationary faculty members demonstrate strong publishing records were now able to do so. Thus, campuses by the hundreds, emboldened by the buyers' market, seized the opportunity to upgrade their faculties by hiring and retaining those who could meet institutional expectations for publishing. While there can be little quarrel with efforts to increase the quality of the faculty, the fact is that a highly consequential, massive trade-off was under way: The teaching mission was being seriously eroded as the culture shifted to embrace scholarly publishing at these aspiring campuses.

As the skew away from teaching became more evident, countervailing forces began to materialize. Critics of the declining condition of undergraduate education were becoming more vocal. In the late 1970s, Harvard's move to revive a core curriculum, under the baton of Henry Rosovsky, gave a boost and legitimacy to curriculum reform that inspired similar efforts at numerous campuses to refashion a more coherent undergraduate curriculum. Report after report in the 1980s urged further reform, both in the curriculum and in teaching. Two reports received more attention than most: *Involvement in Learning: Realizing the Potential of American Higher Education* (Study Group on the Conditions of Excellence in American Higher Education, 1985) and *Integrity in the College Curriculum: A Report to the Academic Community* (Association of American Colleges, 1985). In a related development, the quality of teaching by graduate assistants came under attack, sometimes by accountability-minded state legislators.

Prodded by external critics and regional accreditors, the campus-based proponents of reform took up an ambitious agenda. In the span of a very few years, assessment and outcomes measures catapulted to prominence among national association and campus priorities. In the process, the movement to resuscitate teaching gathered momentum. One encouraging facet has been the more systematic efforts to improve the effectiveness of teaching assistants. By 1990, the bold arguments of Ernest Boyer and R. Eugene Rice to reconceptualize what constituted legitimate "scholarship"—in ways that would better legitimate teaching-related activities other than research leading to publication—contributed additional impetus to the reform movement (Boyer, 1990).

The net result of this tangle of activity is not easy to measure. On the one hand, only the most cynical critics would deny that some movement toward the restoration of teaching has taken place. However, the grip of an enduring research-tilted reward system for faculty is still very much in evidence at all types of institutions, except for the community colleges (Fairweather, in press). In any event, few would contend that undergraduate education in general or that teaching more specifically has attained satisfactory levels. This teaching-deficit condition presents a formidable challenge to graduate schools: to think more creatively about what graduate education should and can do to better prepare future generations of professors.

Enhanced Role of Graduate School

My second proposition holds that graduate schools *should* play a much more prominent role in the preparation of those who aspire to become faculty members. This argument is based on a threefold premise: First, graduate education succeeds admirably in training would-be professors in the ways of doing research and by providing, largely by osmosis, models of what professors actually do in their many-faceted professional lives. Second, many neophyte faculty members are inadequately prepared to teach, and fewer still have an informed vision of the academic profession and the complex culture and institutions that professors inhabit. Third, graduate education does a poor job in two crucial respects: facilitating effective training for teaching and, even more neglected, providing perspective about the values and norms of academic life.

Academic departments indisputably play the dominant role in transmitting the body of knowledge and the research methodologies vital to graduate students' preparation. But beyond that, what is accomplished on campuses to prepare future teachers-scholars? On most campuses, I fear that the answer is very little, for many—probably most—doctorate-granting institutions do not succeed in two critical domains: training graduate students to become effective teachers (although some progress in recent years, as noted, is evident) and familiarizing them with the larger issues of academic organization and the academic profession. In all, campus efforts in general, and graduate school efforts in particular, appear to be seriously inadequate.

Teaching. First, consider teaching. A national study of teaching assistants (TAs)—the first of its kind—established a point of departure several years ago: "Teaching assistants are not only responsible for a major portion of undergraduate lower division instruction at most major research universities, but they are also the potential faculty members of tomorrow. Unfortunately, there is a general perception that the teaching performance of many teaching assistants is poor" (Diamond and Gray, 1987, p. 1). It is unfortunate that a problem so important, so widely acknowledged, seems to have received so little attention within the academy. Students complain regularly about poor teaching. Horror stories occasionally surface. Of course, not all TAs and new faculty members are inadequately prepared. The evidence suggests otherwise: Most of them, in fact, appear to do reasonably well in meeting their demanding mix of responsibilities. But surely the need exists for substantial improvement.

The results of Diamond and Gray's (1987) survey deserve close attention: Seventy-five percent of 1,357 TAs at eight major research universities (six public, two private) reported that they hoped to teach full-time or part-time after they graduated. Close to 20 percent of the TAs reported that they were not getting adequate guidance and supervision from the department or college in which they taught (1987, pp. 36–41). About 20 percent of the respondents reported that they were not given enough time to adequately fulfill their teaching responsibilities (pp. 30–33). And high proportions of TAs reported that they desired more training in such areas as how to evaluate themselves as teachers (72 percent), how to evaluate their courses (71 percent), lecturing (60 percent), conducting classroom discussions (55 percent), using media (54 percent), and preparing texts (53 percent) (pp. 52–53). The evidence may be inconclusive, but numerous indicators from that benchmark survey and subsequent studies suggest that preparation for teaching has been at best uneven and, on balance, can be characterized as shaky.

Professionalization. Graduate training inevitably provides a strong measure of socialization to the discipline—the so-called invisible college. But that process obscures the importance of the larger, too-often-neglected socialization experience, namely, acculturation to the more general norms of the academic profession. As LaPidus (1987, p. 3) has observed, "In most cases the relationship to the discipline . . . is inherent; that to the university is incidental." There are many elements of academic life that bear examination in graduate school. While the invisible college affords a rigorous course of intradisciplinary instruction and provides, in part through osmosis, an introduction to the extradepartmental norms of academe, it is not enough. There is much with which professors-to-be can and should become familiar during their period of preparation, matters that transcend the boundaries of academic departments. There is much more to becoming a professor than to becoming a competent anthropologist, engineer, historian, or microbiologist.

The main barriers are twofold: doubts about content and method. Academe remains highly skeptical about the proposition that there is a corpus of useful, relevant information and concepts about the academy and academic careers that should be passed on to neophytes. As to method, the problem is compounded by the rejection of the notion that such matters can be taught authoritatively, usefully, and effectively. The skeptics' biases are not without foundation; the goal of conveying insights about the richly nuanced academy and about multifaceted academic careers is not easily achieved. But the multifaceted study of higher education and knowledge about the enterprise, including the teaching-learning process, have advanced. A corpus of relevant material exists, and it can be conveyed in useful ways to would-be professors. Useful models do exist.

Countermeasures. What might be done to redress these shortcomings? Graduate schools should initiate efforts aimed at assessing the extent to which problems exist and at helping to launch programs designed to respond to those problems. Some graduate schools already have significant programs in place; most do not. Thus, assuming that no other unit on campus already is playing a major campuswide role, the graduate school should initiate a coordinated program designed to help better prepare prospective professors.

What, then, are the desirable elements of such a program? Consider five aspects of a coordinated effort:

Assessment of Teaching Preparedness. Campuses should make a serious effort to assess the effectiveness of their TAs and to identify specific problems for which help is needed. Such an effort might utilize the questionnaire developed by Diamond and Gray (1987) for their national study of TAs. An effort should be made as well to determine whether TAs have adequate access to whatever teaching improvement facilities exist on campus.

Intervention. It is important to develop special seminars for prospective faculty members. Such seminars probably ought to be required of all TAs by their respective departments and strongly encouraged for others who are contemplating academic careers. Models come in all shapes and sizes, for example, a two-seminar sequence offered by the Teaching Resource Center at the University of California, Davis, and a four-course specialty in college teaching offered at Florida State University.

The content of such seminars ought to address major issues in the teaching-learning process. Useful topics might include lecturing, guiding class discussion, counseling and advising, evaluation, test construction, ethical issues, teaching critical thinking, and so forth. But these topics are not enough. Such seminars, ideally, should seek to acquaint participants with basic information about American higher education and the academic profession. This effort might include modules on the history of American colleges and universities and the evolution of their missions, on the basic elements of organization and governance, on the differences among types of institutions, and on the academic profession. These seminars should examine some of the major policy statements of the American Association of University Professors that establish principles of academic freedom and shared governance. Other segments might broach such topics as the financing of higher education, the relationship of the public policy process to postsecondary education, and the rudiments of the academic labor market. I believe that a great many faculty members are largely unfamiliar with many of these topics, and that ignorance of them is widespread among graduate students.

Another essential element of the preparation process is to familiarize the neophytes about diversity among learners in American higher education. I have already mentioned diversity among types of institutions. Now I refer to the diversity in students' learning styles. This is a topic that a good many current faculty members would do well to take up. Consider for a moment the tidal shifts, in a remarkably short span of time, in the characteristics of postsecondary education students. The full-time white male student, in residence at a four-year institution, was the norm—or certainly he was the modal student—at a time when a large proportion of today's faculty members began their academic careers. Today, however, that norm has faded into the pages of history. More specifically, among contemporary postsecondary students, half attend on a part-time basis; more than half are women (one remarkable datum: by 1989, for the first time, over half of the Ph.D.'s, excluding science and engineering, earned by U.S. citizens were earned by women); only two-fifths of all students are age twenty-one or under; and about one-seventh are not white, which is about two-and-a-half times the proportion in 1960. In all, no more than one in six college and university students actually fits the traditional mold so prominent only two decades ago.

Moreover, by almost any measure, the level of preparation of college students has slipped badly. Judging by standardized test scores, we can see that Scholastic Aptitude Test verbal scores are down a full half of a standard deviation since 1960—that is, about fifty points—and the mathematics scores on this test have dipped significantly as well. (These numbers tell only part of the story, for part of the decline is attributable to the larger proportions of students taking the standardized examinations.) Concomitantly, student interests in fields of study have shifted dramatically in the past decade and a half. Many fewer students today enter college with an affinity for liberal learning.

So, large proportions of today's students are nontraditional. What are we doing to accommodate these new learners? The answer appears to be not very much insofar as the preparation of future professors is concerned. Thus, concentrated attention needs to be paid to these new learners, especially to older students, ethnic minorities, and part-timers. There are critically important lessons for would-be faculty members to learn about teaching strategies designed to engage these learners more effectively. And what better place to start than for graduate schools to encourage and facilitate at least some measure of orientation to the new realities for the next generation of teacher-scholars?

Certification. Certificates of some sort should be awarded to those who complete an appropriate training program. The purpose is not to certify that a graduate student is thereby qualified to be a professor or is somehow certified to be a competent teacher. No sequence of seminars would, or should, suffice for such purposes. Rather, the purposes would be to signal to aspirants to academic careers that the campus takes the preparation role seriously and to provide some evidence to prospective employers that a graduate student has had at least some systematic exposure to the topics of effective teaching and the culture and organization of higher education.

Evaluation. Whatever activities exist or are created to improve the pedagogical skills of future professors, a systematic effort to evaluate the effectiveness of those programs is critically important.

Recruitment. Campuses should also mount activities to encourage those highly able undergraduates who will have a range of attractive career choices to entertain seriously the prospect of an academic career. There are many ways to expose excellent undergraduates to the positive aspects of academic life; among them, opportunities to collaborate with faculty members in research activities can provide rich insights. Also, a series of faculty panels and talks on the joys (and frustrations) of academic life could be quite useful in influencing talented students to consider seriously an academic career.

The five areas outlined above illustrate the kinds of activities that graduate schools might promote and facilitate, even take operational responsibility for, depending on local circumstances.

Graduate Schools' Ability to Make a Difference

But *can* it be done? Can graduate schools really make a difference? This question brings me to my third proposition, that graduate schools can, in fact, make a substantial contribution in the preparation of the next generation of teacher-scholars.

Realism requires acknowledging that graduate deans and graduate schools (or graduate divisions) are in some respects anomalies. Like everything else in the sprawling, decentralized higher education enterprise, the organization and influence of graduate-level education come in endless variations. Ordinarily, however, the graduate sector is seriously constrained in its ability to shape such fundamentals as curriculum and academic personnel matters, and its influence over campus research policies varies markedly from one campus to another. Accordingly, there should be no illusion that graduate schools possess magic wands that can be waved to generate fresh resources or to readily transform campus practices that bear on the preparation of future generations of professors. Decentralization and diffused influence are cornerstones of graduate education.

It is widely assumed that academic preparation ought to be left in the hands of academic departments. This conviction is grounded in the reality that the disciplines have different cultures, values, methods, and labor market patterns (Clark, 1987). Accordingly, strategies that rely heavily on centralized, campuswide approaches to the preparation of professors are often deemed irrelevant. In other words, there are numerous obstacles to an influential graduate school role in these matters.

Conceding that these barriers tend to thwart a robust graduate school role, I submit that graduate schools, nonetheless, have the means to accomplish much more to redress glaring shortcomings in preparing tomorrow's faculty members. Speaking to the role of graduate schools, LaPidus (1987, p. 10) has noted that "TAs are part of the undergraduate teaching force, and department chairmen as well as college deans may feel that graduate deans have no business interfering in what is basically an undergraduate instructional issue. But if the issue is defined in terms of the preparation of future faculty members, it becomes the business of all those to whom the continuing quality and vitality of the faculty is important." Graduate school leadership is well situated to address the problems at hand for five reasons:

Legitimacy. The compartmentalized organization of universities means that few offices have a scope of responsibility that transcends the more parochial interests of the departments and colleges that comprise the university. On the other hand, the graduate school or division cuts across those boundaries. Its purview is graduate education; it possesses inherent legitimacy for addressing graduate education writ large. It necessarily shares in the responsibility for preparing future professors, from anthropology to zoology. The key question is the following: To what degree will the graduate school act on its legitimate authority?

Familiarity. Graduate schools have no monopoly of information about preparation-related issues, and no special wisdom about effective countermeasures. Even so, their placement in the organization spans the many subcultures and realities of the academy; their vantage point affords familiarity with the nature and dimensions of the preparation problem.

Modulated Role. Every graduate school setting is idiosyncratic; no single formula is conceivable to describe an appropriate or normative graduate school role. On some campuses, the graduate school can take operational responsibility for some programs designed to prepare professors more effectively; on others, the appropriate role—possibly, the only acceptable role—is limited to that of a facilitator, catalyst, and, of course, advocate. Thus, the graduate school role will inevitably vary from campus to campus, but the minimally appropriate role surely is to encourage and facilitate significant activities.

Timeliness. With the succession of reports underscoring the shortcomings of undergraduate teaching, the time is ripe for graduate schools to become more creative in preparing more effectively the future corps of college and university faculty members.

Leadership Vacuum. Leadership on campus commonly is lacking to address issues of preparation across the campus. On most campuses, a veritable vacuum exists so far as these issues are concerned, and the graduate school is well positioned to act to fill the void.

In sum, graduate schools are neither powerless to influence the complex environment in which they exist nor incapable of formulating and facilitating realistic programs to address pressing needs. They need to become more involved, minimally as effective advocates, catalysts, and facilitators and, depending on the latitude afforded them locally, take operational responsibility as well.

Urgency Dictated by the Academic Labor Market

My fourth and final proposition holds that the academic labor market will be undergoing a major transformation, an upheaval that makes it imperative for graduate schools to assume now a prominent role in the responsibilities to which I have referred. To understand this situation, we need to comprehend the dimensions of supply and demand.

The faculty that is now in place is almost certainly the best qualified (by traditional measures) ever to inhabit our campuses. Moreover, although relatively few new full-time faculty members have been hired in recent years, recruits on the whole have been very good. However, considerable evidence indicates that by decade's end colleges and universities will find it very hard to attract a sufficient number of highly capable individuals into academic careers.

The declining interest in academic careers in the 1970s and 1980s can be explained in part by the small number of tenure-track academic appointments that have been available. As the number of appointments begins to increase, academic careers will undoubtedly become more attractive to able young people. But it is apparent that, unless the academic profession undergoes other changes as well, a considerable proportion of those talented undergraduates who would have pursued academic careers in former times will not opt to do so now. Thus, the challenge with respect to supply is not only to generate sufficient numbers but also, quantity aside, to attract to academic careers persons of suitable quality.

With respect to the demand side of the equation, it is the huge gap between supply and demand, shortly to emerge, that will create a problem with very serious consequences for the United States. Several hundred thousand academic appointments will have to be made between now and the year 2010 in order to fill anticipated vacancies (Bowen and Schuster, 1986; Bowen and Sosa, 1989). This surge in the number of openings will be a function of two parallel developments: first, retirements, as the large cohort of current faculty members hired during the explosive period of growth in the 1950s and 1960s reaches retirement age, and, second, an anticipated upswing in college enrollments in the mid-1990s, when the baby boomlet now affecting elementary and middle schools reaches college age. Most of the new faculty hiring will be compressed into the fifteen-year period between 1995 and 2010, since relatively few openings will materialize in most fields prior to 1995.

Two important complexities have made difficult the task of estimating the number of openings: The first complexity is the passage of legislation in 1986 that lifts the cap off mandatory retirement ages. This provision takes effect for faculty members in January 1994, at roughly the same time that the overall demand for faculty will be rising. When the cap lifts, if pension plans do not afford faculty members reasonable retirement incomes, many faculty members presumably will choose to continue in their jobs beyond age seventy. This "X factor" could limit the number of new hires. However, the available evidence, drawn from venues where state laws or institutional policies have raised or uncapped altogether a mandatory retirement age, shows that the vast majority of faculty will continue to retire around age sixty-five (Rees and Smith, 1991). The second complexity is the current budget crisis that grips many states. Along with the severely imbalanced federal budget, budgetary constraints serve to limit resources available to replace retiring faculty.

The need for new appointments will pose a formidable challenge to the academic community. The entire U.S. faculty numbers about 485,000 full-time members and another 220,000 or so part-timers. Therefore, the hiring of several hundred thousand new faculty members in a short span of time amounts to the replacement of a sizable proportion of the existing professoriate. In all, the urgency of developing an adequate supply of well-prepared faculty members to meet future demand may constitute the most consequential of all of the challenges confronting the academic profession.

To complicate this awesome task further, higher education in the United States is faced with the vitally important but very difficult task of attracting a much larger number of ethnic minorities to academic careers. Unless we succeed in doing so, our institutions of higher education will be staffed by a faculty that lags ever further behind in reflecting the growing cultural diversity of our society. Unless present trends are sharply reversed, our colleges and universities will drift further and further away from their responsibility to field faculties that better mirror the larger society.

What all of this means is that graduate programs will be looked on to prepare many thousands of faculty members in the proximate future—more, in fact, in a short period of time than has been the case since the 1960s and arguably more than ever before. Unless we begin now to create and sustain a multidimensional program of preparation for the future cohort of professors, we shall be channeling thousands of ill-prepared graduate students into the nation's college classrooms.

Conclusion

In sum, as higher education moves toward a period of massive hiring, graduate schools must be open to supplementing the academic departments' dominant role in transmitting the body of knowledge and research methodologies crucial to the preparation of new professors. Graduate schools have a key role to play in harnessing the capacities of the campuses to teach about higher education, to transmit the ethos of the academic workplace, and to pass on the culture and the ethics of the profession. This role, though supplemental, should not be viewed as incidental; it should not be seen as an optional add-on only if ample resources somehow materialize.

Precisely how a particular graduate school might define and implement its role will, of course, vary considerably from one setting to another. Much work lies just ahead in preparing the many thousands of new entrants into academic careers. Toward that end, the potential contribution of graduate schools, extending beyond the prevailing custom of great deference to academic departments, is enormous.

References

Association of American Colleges. *Integrity in the College Curriculum: A Report to the Academic Community.* Washington, D.C.: Association of American Colleges, 1985.

Bowen, H. R., and Schuster, J. H. *American Professors: A National Resource Imperiled.* New York: Oxford University Press, 1986.

Bowen, W. G., and Sosa, J. A. *Prospects for Faculty in the Arts and Sciences.* Princeton, N.J.: Princeton University Press, 1989.

Boyer, E. L. *Scholarship Reconsidered: Priorities of the Professoriate.* Princeton, N.J.: Princeton University Press, 1990.

Clark, B. R. *Academic Life: Small Worlds, Different Worlds.* Princeton, N.J.: Carnegie Foundation for the Advancement of Teaching, 1987.

Diamond, R. M., and Gray, P. *National Study of Teaching Assistants.* Syracuse, N.Y.: Center for Instructional Development, Syracuse University, 1987.

Fairweather, J. "Faculty Reward Structures: Toward Institutional and Professional Homogeneity." *Research in Higher Education,* in press.

LaPidus, J. B. "The Role of Graduate Education in the Preparation of Faculty." Paper presented at the annual National Conference on Higher Education, American Association for Higher Education, Chicago, March 1987.

Rees, A., and Smith, S. P. *Faculty Retirement in the Arts and Sciences.* Princeton, N.J.: Princeton University Press, 1991.

Study Group on the Conditions of Excellence in American Higher Education. National Institute of Education. *Involvement in Learning: Realizing the Potential of American Higher Education.* Washington, D.C.: Government Printing Office, 1985.

JACK H. SCHUSTER *is professor of education and public policy at Claremont Graduate School, Claremont, California, and has been a visiting scholar at the University of Michigan, Brookings Institution, and Oxford University.*

If the faculty of the future is to reflect diverse talents and perspectives, it is important to find a way to include a diversity of people in graduate programs. To do so, we need to value and nurture alternative voices and different ways of knowing. By opening education to a broader range of scholarship, we can begin to honor the multiple voices.

To Hear All Voices: A Broader View of Faculty Scholarship

Laurie Richlin

Impending Crisis and Opportunity

As the cohort of predominantly white, male faculty hired in the boom years of the late 1950s and early 1960s reaches retirement age, the demand for new faculty will skyrocket (Bowen and Schuster, 1986; Bowen and Sosa, 1989; Atkinson, 1990; Mooney and Blum, 1990; Holden, 1990; Burke, 1988; Blum, 1990). It is estimated that the graying of current faculty will require the replacement of up to a half million positions during the next few decades, with up to 340,000 of those replacements needed by the year 2004 (Jack H. Schuster, in Johnson, 1990). The actual rate of faculty turnover is "still low but increasing . . . somewhat higher than the long-term patterns estimated by Bowen and Schuster in the 1986 study" (El-Khawas, 1990, p. 3).

In addition to faculty retirement, institutions also need to hire new faculty because of "changes in enrollment, new academic programs and emerging areas of research inquiry" (El-Khawas, 1990, p. 1). That is, a different sort of faculty person, able to teach the increasingly diverse student population and prepared for scholarship in interdisciplinary areas, will be required in order to meet the needs of colleges and universities (Ann Austin, in Johnson, 1990). El-Khawas reported in 1990 that "most colleges and universities (60 percent) increased the number of women among their faculty in the past year" and "four in 10 institutions reported a net gain in the number of their faculty from under-represented racial/ethnic groups" (p. 2). There is no doubt then, as B. Claude Mathis has observed, that "the greatest investment an institution of higher education makes during the

NEW DIRECTIONS FOR TEACHING AND LEARNING, no. 54, Summer 1993 © Jossey-Bass Publishers

coming decades may well be the hiring of new faculty members" (Whitt, 1991, p. 177).

Institutions already are reporting problems in filling these positions, "particularly in certain high-demand disciplines" (El-Khawas, 1990, p. viii; Atkinson, 1990), well before the projected wave of retirements occurs. For instance, in mathematical sciences, "By the year 1993, the projected number of retirements in mathematics faculty at America's colleges will exceed the present annual number of U.S. citizens who receive a Ph.D. in the mathematical sciences. By 1997, the number of retirements will exceed the total number of Ph.D.s—U.S. and foreign—in the mathematical sciences" (Kirwan, 1990, p. 23). The majority of all types of institutions have reported that in at least a few fields it is taking them "longer to find qualified persons" and that they have had "greater difficulty in getting top applicants to accept positions" (El-Khawas, 1990, p. 23). Research-oriented Ph.D.'s have greater opportunities now to work outside academe (Atkinson, 1990; Kirwan, 1990), and there is increasing competition with "industry, government and other nonprofit employers in trying to hire persons with advanced training" (El-Khawas, 1990, p. 1).

In 1990, I surveyed the chairs in four types of departments (biology, history, mathematics, and psychology) and the graduate or academic deans in 251 institutions stratified by Carnegie classification (see Carnegie Foundation for the Advancement of Teaching, 1987) and type of support (private or public) (Richlin, 1991). The sample then was divided into two categories: those schools with graduate programs awarding the Ph.D. (called "providers" of new faculty) and those that did not award the Ph.D. (called "consumers"). Of the respondents, over half of the consumer institutions reported hiring difficulties during the prior few years. All institutions surveyed anticipated having more difficulty in the next three to five years, with more than 59 percent of all institutions anticipating hiring problems within ten years. Many of the respondents had heard that there would be fewer graduate students coming through the graduate school pipeline at the same time retirements were expected, and they anticipated difficulty whether or not they had already experienced a shortage in applicants. Some of the respondents reported concerns about finding minority faculty and finding the finances to pay competitive salaries and provide needed resources. Several graduate school deans in the survey mentioned tight markets in fields such as management and computer science that have high outside competition for Ph.D.'s.

There were both generalized and specific concerns expressed by respondents who reported current or anticipated difficulties in hiring qualified college teachers. A primary concern for all was the number of students entering the graduate school pipeline, particularly minorities and, in the sciences, English speakers. Although chairs of departments that awarded Ph.D.'s worried about attracting top-notch researchers, department chairs at liberal arts and comprehensive colleges were more concerned about finding faculty with breadth in their fields and ability to teach their subjects.

Biology chairs in provider schools cited lack of resources to attract high-quality faculty, primarily researchers. One stated that "this is a 'research' university. Teaching is a nuisance or necessary evil." At consumer schools, biology chairs had much different concerns: "Very few candidates seem capable or willing to teach introductory or nonmajors' courses, which form the backbone of our department. We are quite interdisciplinary and focused on teaching. Too many are seeking research refuge." "There are not enough broadly educated biologists—too highly specialized."

The same division of concerns was expressed by history, mathematics, and psychology department chairs in the study. In non-doctorate-granting departments, the following concerns were typical: "For small departments, breadth of preparation is as important as depth. Graduate schools need to pay attention to the 'generalist' market." "Finding teachers who can teach in a broad interdisciplinary program and bring disciplinary expertise." "Too many candidates are narrow specialists without disciplinary breadth, inter-disciplinary capability, and teaching experience." "We are required to hire Ph.D.'s, and the applicants we have had recently have, to a large extent, not had the commitment to teaching which I would like to see." "Difficult to find people who can communicate well with students, establish rapport with students, and who have a broad background in mathematics." "Small college teaching (twelve credits per semester) is not attractive to new graduates. Few really want to teach, and certainly not this many courses or sections." "Our curriculum is four-year liberal arts. Finding someone with diversity of interest, research experience, and teaching skills is difficult."

Only 36.7 percent of provider institutions agreed that there was not enough teacher training in graduate school, compared to 86.4 percent of consumer institutions. Doctorate-granting department chairs were almost evenly split between agreeing (51.7 percent) and disagreeing (48.3 percent) that graduate students get enough information about the professional roles of faculty, while non-doctorate-granting department chairs overwhelmingly agreed that the students do not get enough of this information (80.1 percent). Only 19.6 percent of providers agreed that their institutions, departments, or disciplines stressed research and research training at the cost of properly preparing college teachers, compared with 72.3 percent of consumers who agreed with the statement.

Selection Process

As a result of their research-focused selection process, graduate schools have been "recruiting the 'wrong' people for the professoriate—people who can't teach well and, in fact, would rather not teach at all" (Bess, 1990, p. 20). The current "pool of would-be teachers is . . . filled with people whose innate character is not likely to make them good teachers" (p. 21). As stated by the vice president of a non-doctorate-granting university, "Often we recruit new faculty members as if we were Harvard. Seldom do we consciously try to seek out faculty members who want to be at the institutions we represent. . . . This, in turn, often means that there is no sense of pride for either their institution or their role in it" (Boyer, 1990, p. 61). Approximately two-thirds of the provider institutions in my study (Richlin, 1991) disagreed (while 57.5 percent of the consumers agreed) that their institutions do not do a good job of initial selection of people who would be good college teachers when admitting applicants into their Ph.D. programs. Comments from providers included "Not a criterion at admissions," "Not even taken into account," "We don't select on that basis," and "Why should we select future teachers?" Comments from consumer departments included "Impossible!" "Many programs actively discourage people from a teaching position," "But is that their job?" "Probably only interested in research dollars," and "I don't know whether they fail to attract good ones or destroy good ones that they attract."

The call for a return to teaching undergraduates gives an unprecedented opportunity to select and prepare individuals interested in becoming teacher-scholars, rather than rely on the traditional graduates of doctoral programs structured on the basis of research ability alone. The recruitment of enough high-quality graduate students suitable to be college teachers depends on finding teaching-oriented students who are not predisposed to narrow, disciplinary investigation (Katz and Hartnett, 1976).

New Models of Graduate Education

Models of graduate education are still being proposed to help "young scholars" learn the "nature and responsibilities of teaching and . . . [help] them develop their talents" (Stanley, 1989, p. 8) and to reward a broader range of practice (Watkins, 1990; Clifford, 1990). Cartter's (1967) "track system," which separates those going into college teaching from other Ph.D.'s, has been reproposed by Ivar Stakgold and Stephen Rodi for preparing mathematics professors (Jackson, 1990, pp. 266–267) and by several others for all future faculty (see, for example, Fitzgerald, 1989; Edgerton, 1990). Rodi contends that "an isolated course in teaching is not going to do much good" (Jackson, 1990, p. 267). Fitzgerald (1989, pp. 3–4) would require "those graduate students working toward the Ph.D. and having aspirations to teach in college and universities . . . [to] complete course work in the professional education areas of instructional methods and techniques, human development and learning, educational philosophy, and a teaching internship or practicum," with, as the only benefit to the graduate, a note on the transcript indicating "an additional concentration in professional education courses." Edgerton (1990, p. 9) visualizes a "teaching residency" at a liberal arts college while the graduate student is working on the dissertation half-time, and "grand [teaching] rounds" for "teaching residents."

Schön (1983, 1987) has introduced the concept of the reflective practitioner, who acts more like a researcher trying to model a system than an expert being modeled. This knowing-in-action entails the "paradox of learning a really new competence," wherein "a student cannot at first understand what he needs to learn, can learn it only by educating himself, and can educate himself only by beginning to do what he does not understand" (1983, p. 83). This characterization certainly applies to learning to teach.

As I noted in Chapter One (this volume), the perceived need for a bolder view of the varied tasks of undergraduate teachers is not new. Hollis (1945, pp. 96–97) claimed that graduate education of teachers should be an "all-university function," bringing together the talents of many disciplines, as was being done at the time by Northwestern in its Ed.D. program and at the University of Chicago for its universitywide Ph.D. Vlastos (1980) noted that the shortcomings of preparation for college teaching could not be remedied with courses on teaching methods or supervised teaching alone, that the whole of graduate education had to be diversified and enriched. He suggested that the first two years after the master's degree be disciplinary courses and lead to the preliminary examinations. For the third year, he suggested branching into other fields by taking courses in other departments and even traveling to other campuses for "cultural enrichment" (1980, p. 76).

Van Cleve (1987) recognized that "faculties of Ph.D.-granting departments must climb attitudinal mountains" (p. 19) if the system is going to change because "the emerging Ph.D. stands on the wrong side of a very wide gap" (p. 18). Faculty still "pay a high price" to be undergraduate teachers, according to Lacey (1990, p. B3). In the past, he says, ignorance led to poor preparation; today, the same preparation "can only be willful." How can we "continue to socialize future professors according to a false model?" he asks. There must be a new model that supports the "growth of current faculty members and also helps prepare future ones" (p. B3).

New Vision of Scholarship

In an attempt to reframe the debate between research and teaching, the Carnegie Foundation for the Advancement of Teaching has suggested a multidimensional scholarship with four components: discovery, integration, application, and teaching (Boyer, 1990). Discovery, the search for new facts or the creation of new knowledge and theory, has been a traditional part of graduate education in the form of the dissertation, as Hamilton (this volume) discusses. However, the other three forms of scholarship have not been considered legitimate and significant ways of knowing.

The scholarship of integration, the synthesis of disparate views and disciplines, looks for new relationships and makes the kind of scholarly connections that create meaning from facts. Blaisdell (this volume) describes the rationale for integration of disciplines and the implications of interdisciplinary education on faculty, curriculum, students, and the institution.

The scholarship of application involves reflection on practice and the creation of new paradigms of professional competence. Rice (1992, p. 125) calls this the "most distinctly American" form of scholarship, developed from the great nineteenth-century land grant institutions. However, the scholarship of practice lost its pragmatic roots when the professional schools became part of the university and adopted the academy's emphasis on science. Rice and Richlin (Chapter Seven, this volume) dispute the view that research and theory stand in hierarchically superior relation to practice and argue that application of knowledge to societal problems should be acknowledged as scholarship.

The scholarship of teaching includes representation of knowledge, creation of new ways to draw a field together, and new ways to connect knower and learner. Ronkowski (this volume) describes the developmental stages in becoming a pedagogical scholar and shows how teaching experience during graduate school can enable new college teachers to develop the three elements that Boyer (1990) and Rice (1990, 1992) have identified as part of the scholarship of teaching: synoptic capacity, pedagogical content knowledge, and teaching-learning theory.

Boyer (1990) has called for having all four types of scholarship active within American higher education institutions, suggesting that individual schools could specialize in particular scholarships, or that faculty members could focus on different scholarships during various stages of their careers. Rather than seeing integration, application, and pedagogy as what faculty do in addition to "real" scholarship, Rice (1990, p. 1) has argued that "these other forms of scholarship—these other ways of knowing—are as legitimate, significant, and needed as the dominant mode." He has acknowledged that the new scholarship "challenges a hierarchical arrangement of monumental proportions—a status system that is firmly fixed in the consciousness of the present faculty and the academy's organizational policies and practices," but he calls for "a broader, more open field where these different forms of scholarship can interact, inform, and enrich one another, and faculty can follow their interests, build on their strengths, and be rewarded for what they spend most of their scholarly energy doing" (1990, p. 2).

Conclusion

To hear all of the voices that reflect the diverse talents and perspectives of the U.S. citizenry, it is important to broaden the range of scholarship in our colleges and universities. New visions of scholarship depend on the recognition of the different aspects of faculty work as intellectually important. That recognition, in addition to the selection of promising graduate students and appropriate graduate education, is necessary whether the solution to scholarly diversity is to have each higher education institution choose a particular type of scholarship in which to excel, to have departments attempt to find a range of talent in the faculty that they hire, or to have individual faculty members explore different scholarships over the course of their careers. Even with departmental reward systems designed to encourage a wide range of faculty activities, if graduate students are not selected, motivated, and educated to do other than narrow discovery-type research, we shall still hear only a single voice. To cultivate a diverse faculty, we need to begin at the beginning: determine the need for alternative scholarships and design programs to educate the faculty of the future.

References

Atkinson, R. C. "Supply and Demand for Scientists and Engineers: A National Crisis in the Making." *Science,* 1990, *248,* 425–432.

Bess, J. L. "College Teachers: Miscast Professionals." *Change,* May–June 1990, pp. 19–22.

Blum, D. E. "More Moderate Increase in Faculty Retirements Predicted in New Study." *Chronicle of Higher Education,* April 4, 1990, pp. A1, A16.

Bowen, H. R., and Schuster, J. H. *American Professors: A National Resource Imperiled.* New York: Oxford University Press, 1986.

Bowen, W. G., and Sosa, J. A. *Prospects for Faculty in the Arts and Sciences.* Princeton, N.J.: Princeton University Press, 1989.

Boyer, E. L. *Scholarship Reconsidered: Priorities of the Professoriate.* Princeton, N.J.: Princeton University Press, 1990.

Burke, D. L. *A New Academic Marketplace.* New York: Greenwood Press, 1988.

Carnegie Foundation for the Advancement of Teaching. *A Classification of Institutions of Higher Education.* Princeton, N.J.: Princeton University Press, 1987.

Cartter, A. M. "Future Faculty: Needs and Resources." In C.B.T. Lee (ed.), *Improving College Teaching.* Washington, D.C.: American Council on Education, 1967.

Clifford, G. J. " 'Let Hayward State Do It . . . ?' " *Review of Higher Education,* 1990, *13* (3), 387–396.

Edgerton, R. "The Making of a Professor." Paper presented at the annual National Conference on Higher Education, American Association for Higher Education, San Francisco, April 1990.

El-Khawas, E. *Campus Trends, 1990.* Higher Education Panel Reports, no. 80. Washington, D.C.: American Council on Education, 1990.

Fitzgerald, R. G. "The Teaching Doctorate: A Need for Teaching Credentials in Higher Education." *The PEN,* September–October 1989, pp. 3–5.

Holden, C. "Ph.D. Squeeze." *Science,* 1990, *247,* 406.

Hollis, E. V. *Toward Improving Ph.D. Programs.* Washington, D.C.: American Council on Education, 1945.

Jackson, A. "Graduate Education in Mathematics: Is It Working?" *Notices of the American Mathematical Society,* 1990, *37,* 266–268.

Johnson, R. C. "Faculty Exchange Meeting: Issues of the 90s." Internal memorandum to provost staff, Miami University, Oxford, Ohio, Nov. 26, 1990.

Katz, J., and Hartnett, R. T. "Recommendations for Training Better Scholars." In J. Katz and R. T. Hartnett (eds.), *Scholars in the Making*. New York: Ballinger, 1976.

Kirwan, W. E. "Meeting the Mathematical Needs of Our Nation's Work Force." *Educational Horizons*, 1990, *69* (1), 22–27.

Lacey, P. A. "Let's Not Perpetuate Our Mistakes of the Past as We Prepare a New Professorial Generation." *Chronicle of Higher Education*, April 18, 1990, pp. B1, B3.

Mooney, C. J., and Blum, D. E. "A Sampler of Recent Studies of Faculty Demographics." *Chronicle of Higher Education*, Apr. 4, 1990, p. A17.

Rice, R. E. "Rethinking What It Means to Be a Scholar." *Teaching Excellence: Toward the Best in the Academy*, Winter–Spring 1990, pp. 1–2.

Rice, R. E. "Toward a Broader Conception of Scholarship: The American Context." In T. G. Whiston and R. L. Geiger (eds.), *Research and Higher Education in the United Kingdom and the United States*. Lancaster, England: Society for Research into Higher Education, 1992.

Richlin, L. "Preparing Future Faculty: Meeting the Need for Teacher-Scholars by Enlarging the View of Scholarship in Ph.D. Programs." Unpublished doctoral dissertation, Department of Education, Claremont Graduate School, 1991.

Schön, D. A. *The Reflective Practitioner: How Professionals Think in Action*. New York: Basic Books, 1983.

Schön, D. A. *Educating the Reflective Practitioner: Toward a New Design for Teaching and Learning in the Professions*. San Francisco: Jossey-Bass, 1987.

Stanley, P. "Graduate Education and Its Patrons: Foundations." *Council of Graduate Schools Communicator*, 1989, *22* (1), 1–3, 8.

Van Cleve, J. "Graduate Study and Professional Responsibilities." *ADFL Bulletin*, 1987, *18*, 18–19.

Vlastos, G. "Graduate Education in the Humanities." In W. K. Frankena (ed.), *The Philosophy and Future of Graduate Education*. Ann Arbor: University of Michigan Press, 1980.

Watkins, B. T. "New Technique Tested to Evaluate College Teaching." *Chronicle of Higher Education*, May 16, 1990, pp. A15, A17.

Whitt, E. J. " 'Hit The Ground Running': Experiences of New Faculty in a School of Education." *Review of Higher Education*, 1991, *14* (2), 177–197.

LAURIE RICHLIN is interim director of the Office of Research and Evaluation Studies, Antioch College, Yellow Springs, Ohio. She is also executive editor of the Journal on Excellence in College Teaching *and director of the Lilly Conference on College Teaching–West.*

This chapter reviews the place of the dissertation with respect to the adviser-advisee relationship, coursework, and the qualifying examination and considers the qualities of originality, significance, and independence in a changing world of scholarship.

On the Way to the Professoriate: The Dissertation

Russell G. Hamilton

The Dissertation as a Historical Requirement for the Ph.D.

Traditionally, the doctoral dissertation offers definitive proof of students' knowledge of their disciplines, ability to engage in independent research, and ability to present findings in a coherent manner. The dissertation demonstrates that students, by presenting and successfully defending a thesis (that is, a scholarly proposition), merit admission to a defined community of scholars. And, as certified members of that community, the new doctors of philosophy qualify to profess their knowledge.

Since Yale conferred the nation's first Ph.D. in 1861, successive groups of educators and others have taken a keen interest in the role and nature of the dissertation. At no time has that interest been keener than it is today. For many, especially faculty, the very concept of the dissertation is sacrosanct, and its preparation is an often time-consuming and exacting, but necessary, rite of passage. For many others, especially doctoral students, the dissertation is a formidable barrier standing obdurately between the candidate and the degree.

Although many faculty and others see the dissertation as a sacred institution, not to be tampered with, other members of the graduate education community increasingly agree that parts of the process, as well as many of the final products, may be out of step with the academic enterprise and, indeed, with society's overall intellectual and research needs. One of the most frequently heard reasons for this problematic state of the dissertation is that the dissertation contributes, more than anything else, to the inordinate length of time that it takes for so many students to complete the degree,

New Directions for Teaching and Learning, no. 54, Summer 1993 © Jossey-Bass Publishers

particularly in the humanities and social sciences. Moreover, there is a high attrition rate among doctoral candidates, that is, those who have completed all degree requirements but the dissertation (ABDs). Despite the time limit that most graduate schools impose for the completion of the dissertation, it is fairly routine to grant, on petition, one or more extensions to an ABD, even one who reemerges years, sometimes decades, after entering candidacy. In this respect, attrition has an uncertain meaning when applied to the ABD.

Several recently published reports address the main reasons why the final degree requirement so often stands as an insurmountable barrier (Association of American Universities and the Association of Graduate Schools, 1990; Bowen and Rudenstine, 1992; Council of Graduate Schools, 1991b). Almost all of the studies recognize that to an appreciable degree the characteristics of individual disciplines (or groups of disciplines) determine the distinctive role and nature of the dissertation. In this regard, most of the recent studies either suggest or unequivocally state that the dissertation is much more of a problem in the humanities and social sciences than it is in the natural and biomedical sciences and engineering. Whatever the discipline, scientific discoveries, new technologies, the burgeoning and rapid transmission of information, and the expansion and changing contours of knowledge have contributed greatly to the vitality of as well as the concerns surrounding doctoral education in general and the dissertation in particular.

The Dissertation as an Integral Part of Doctoral Education

Depending to some extent on the discipline, we might say that the dissertation is either an integral part or an inevitable outcome of doctoral education. To put it quite simply, when does a student select a topic and initiate research for the dissertation? In most hard science disciplines, for example, it is fairly common for a student to select a topic in the first year of graduate study and immediately initiate research leading to the dissertation. At the other extreme, humanities or social sciences students may not give serious thought to a dissertation topic until they have finished coursework or even entered candidacy. In the case of both sets of students, it behooves us to ask how the years leading up to the actual writing of the dissertation relate to that culminating event.

Adviser-Advisee Relationship. One firm consensus to emerge from the broad-based discussion among graduate students, faculty, and deans who participated in the Council of Graduate School's (CGS, 1991b) project on the dissertation is that a key factor in the successful completion of the degree is the relationship between the adviser and advisee. Whether or not a student identifies a dissertation topic early in the graduate career depends in large measure on the adviser. In the dissertation-writing stage, the role of the adviser often can make all the difference as to whether or not students finish in a timely fashion or, for that matter, finish at all. A great deal has been made of and written about the importance of mentorship and the adviser-advisee relationship (see, for example, CGS, 1991a, on good supervisory practice). I underscore, however, that the role of the adviser affects and defines just about every aspect of students' doctoral programs, from coursework to their qualifying examinations, to the conceptualization and production of their dissertations.

Dissertation and Coursework. The humanities and social sciences content courses, normally taken in students' first and second years, often suggest an area in which to do research or even from which to select a dissertation topic. A first- or second-year theory course can give students some notion of the approach and methodology that they might employ in that normally still-far-off dissertation-writing stage. Furthermore, class papers and a thesis submitted for a master's degree on the way to the Ph.D. are practice runs for the actual dissertation.

Members of the task force who oriented the CGS (1991b) study on the role and nature of the dissertation, as well as faculty, students, and administrators from the forty-three universities who participated in the discussions, agreed that coursework in the humanities is only loosely tied to most students' dissertations. Content courses in the humanities and soft social sciences mainly teach students about the discipline, its history, and, in some cases, how to approach its primary and secondary texts. Beginning students in history, for example, are not yet historians. On the other hand, beginning students in molecular biology enter the graduate program already doing science. For the molecular biology students-scientists, coursework is ancillary to the laboratories where they, working side by side with a faculty adviser, actively engage in research.

In seminars, usually taken no earlier than the second year of graduate study, aspiring historians, would-be literary critics, and their fellow humanities students normally sharpen their disciplinary skills and narrow their scopes with respect to areas of research from which dissertation topics might eventually emerge. More often than not, these seminar students are so preoccupied with their qualifying examinations (the next step in an essentially lockstep process) that they and their advisers give only perfunctory, if any, thought to the dissertation. In sum, what is often lacking in the more diachronic doctoral education of the humanities and social sciences, but frequently present in the sciences, is a kind of synchronic interconnectedness among coursework, research, preparation for the qualifying examinations, and the dissertation.

Dissertation and the Qualifying Examination. For many students and their advisers, the dissertation is climactic. Yet, the qualifying examination, whether in the humanities or social or hard sciences, is the event that circumscribes doctoral training. An important disciplinary distinction is that, in the humanities, the dissertation is often tangential, though certainly not incidental, to the process as a formal continuum. In the laboratory-oriented fields, the dissertation is part of a continuum within a holistic process. But for appreciable numbers of students, the qualifying examination often marks the end of a process. Ziolkowski (1990) and others have noted that the ABD's work can almost be considered a degree in itself. The new beginning, which the research for and writing of the dissertation entail, as Bowen and Rudenstine (1992), among others, have pointed out, frequently is a period of isolation for many doctoral candidates in the humanities. Furthermore, for those who have just entered candidacy after several years of coursework, the immediate postexamination period is frequently a time of letdown. Thus, to begin thinking about the dissertation *after* building up to and passing the qualifying examination can be anticlimactic.

Dissertation as a Rite of Passage. Keeping in mind such factors as postexamination withdrawal or doldrums, students' sometimes overly ambitious topics and lofty objectives, and advisers' demands and often overly high expectations, we readily understand why some consider the dissertation to be the most difficult piece of scholarly writing that one ever undertakes. Despite the difficulties, most of those who persevere believe that the ordeal was not only worth it but also necessary: After all, they survived a rite of passage that separates the fit from the unfit.

A few graduate deans and faculty involved in the CGS (1991b) study went so far as to accept the notion that the dissertation stage could serve to screen students out of doctoral programs. Others contended that it was impractical, at best, and inhumane, at worst, to use the dissertation stage for Darwinian selection to eliminate those who had already devoted several years to graduate education. A majority felt that it was a question not just of weeding out those who could not succeed but also of inadvertently discouraging some potentially very capable scholars by subjecting them to an exercise based more on persistence than intellectual ability and creativity.

Dissertation as a Significant and Original Contribution to Knowledge. To what extent does the finished product constitute an original and significant contribution to the storehouse of knowledge? Most dissertations are undeniably of some intellectual and scholarly benefit to those individuals who research and write them. But the substance of most dissertations usually gains scholarly legitimacy only when published. Because the typical dissertation has only minimal, if any, impact on its field, in terms of size, scope, and time of preparation it should be a correspondingly modest undertaking. And just as the words *ambitious* and *outstanding* are not necessarily synonymous, neither are *modest* and *mediocre*. The CGS (1991b) report on the dissertation, reflecting much of the discussion by students, faculty, and deans, contains revealing statements on the matters of originality, significance, and independence. If one of the principal roles of the dissertation is, indeed, to afford students the opportunity to display their ability to engage in independent research and scholarly reportage, the question is whether or not that piece of scholarship is an original and, more important, a significant contribution to the field. In this regard, CGS (1991b, p. 8) quotes one of the deans who participated in the study: "What is original may not be significant and what is significant may not be original."

A dissertation on a minor literary figure, for example, may constitute originality, but rarely does this kind of work make a significant contribution to knowledge. This reality is borne out by an academic culture that implicitly states that certified and practicing scholars may legitimately disregard dissertations in their field or subfield (a matter to which I later return).

The issue, however, may be one of balance with respect to a dissertation's significance and the time that a student takes to produce it. By way of illustration, in a recent competition sponsored by CGS with University Microfilms International (UMI), a graduate student won a prize awarded annually for the outstanding dissertation. At the awards ceremony, the chair of the evaluation committee revealed that this particular student had taken an admittedly long time to complete the dissertation. The chair went on to make what was for some the curious observation that sometimes, as in this particular case, it was worth it to spend years writing a dissertation. A visiting British academic summed up the sentiments of a number of those in attendance when he suggested that even at the risk of not winning the prize, the awardee would have been better off if she had written a less ambitious dissertation in a shorter period of time. She then could have gone on to turn that shorter, more modest dissertation into a perhaps award-deserving book.

Any suggestion that the dissertation, especially in the humanities, should be shorter and generally less ambitious invariably causes some to decry the perceived lowering of standards. The counterargument is that excellent, prize-winning efforts notwithstanding, most dissertations, even those of great length, based on time-consuming, meticulous research, are not particularly significant contributions to knowledge. Such being the case, as the counterargument goes, it is in the best interest of all concerned (especially the student) to view the dissertation as evidence that the author "has made at least a *modest* contribution to knowledge" (emphasis added; Bowen, 1981, p. 31). Similarly, according to one of CGS's (1991b, p. 3) recommendations, "The dissertation is the beginning of one's scholarly work, not its culmination."

The Dissertation as a Publication, a Source of Publications, or Both

In some disciplines, but especially in the humanities and social sciences, recent Ph.D. recipients are expected to extract from their dissertations a few articles for publication in peer-reviewed journals. The culture of some disciplines dictates that eventually these same article writers turn their dissertations into books, published by university presses. There are, of course, those dissertations, almost exclusively in the sciences, that consist of two or more previously published articles. Some faculty in science disciplines point out, however, that lately the imperative of publishing one or more articles increasingly imposes hardships on their Ph.D. students.

Another much-discussed issue among those participating in the CGS (1991b) project was whether the typical dissertation needed to be scaled up or down to qualify as a publishable manuscript. A number of discussants declared that, in raw form, most humanities and social sciences dissertations were not acceptable as book manuscripts. This generally agreed-upon reality led some CGS project participants to declare that students should write books rather than dissertations that then had to be turned into books. Many faculty contended, however, that what makes a dissertation unpublishable is precisely what makes it a useful, culminating student enterprise, with all of its review of the literature, pedantically exhaustive documentation, and often stilted, dissertation-style language.

A few dissertations do sell a few copies, and scholars in the field occasionally cite them in articles and books. (UMI regularly publishes in its newsletter a list of the year's top-selling dissertations.) In the main, those who buy and cite dissertations are other graduate students writing their own dissertations on the same or related subjects. Faculty indeed seem to observe an unwritten law whereby authors of scholarly articles or books need not cite or otherwise refer to a dissertation, even if the latter treats the same topic as that of their work.

The Dissertation and the Challenges of a Changing Scholarly Environment

In many science disciplines, faculty members who received their doctorates a mere decade or so ago stand the risk of commanding obsolete knowledge if they do not keep abreast of the accelerated, sometimes major, changes in their areas of specialization. Even in humanities disciplines, generally believed to change less than the sciences over an equivalent period of time, there have been dramatic breakthroughs in theory and methodology in the last few decades. And in virtually every discipline there is an increase in the number of primary and secondary sources available. Unquestionably, in the 1990s and ensuing decades graduate students who aspire to the professoriate will have to know and master more than did their counterparts of a generation ago. Even many tradition-bound professors of literature, for example, who generally disdain postmodernist methodologies, grudgingly concede that a new Ph.D., in order to compete in the academic job market, needs to be at least conversant with sign system and other contemporary theories, as well as with new approaches such as feminist rereadings of canonical texts.

Increasingly, we hear and read about the expanding and changing canon. If the literary canon is indeed expanding to include the works of previously excluded or marginalized groups such as women and people of color, then we must expect graduate students to attempt to assimilate greater amounts of information. The implication is that not only do apprentice scholars in all disciplines face greater volumes of materials to synthesize and master, but also they must confront an era of shifting paradigms and sometimes stridently conflicting ideologies. Graduate students in search of dissertation topics may find themselves at sea. The fact that graduate students have so much more from which to choose with respect to thesis topics and approaches is both a blessing and a curse. These are exciting and dynamic times in which to research and write dissertations. At the same time, in addition to possible disorientation in a sea of information, students run at least two other potentially discouraging, if not completely immobilizing, risks: failing to gain control over the topic and material and failing to find a suitable, willing, and enthusiastic adviser for a research project that senior faculty may deem too unconventional or controversial.

In the twin categories of the unconventional and controversial is the *risking trend,* especially among feminist scholars, to use accounts of personal experiences as scholarly works. If it has not occurred yet (and it is bound to have occurred somewhere), it is only a matter of time before doctoral candidates submit proposals for autobiographical dissertations. Certain to follow are accusations of self-indulgence and failure to be dispassionately analytical in the manner of rigorous scholarly writing, voiced by skeptical or even outraged faculty members. My intent here is neither to condone nor condemn any particular orthodoxy or unorthodoxy but rather to call for a greater flexibility with respect to the form and content of dissertations as emerging scholars attempt to respond to the demands of expanding areas of knowledge and changing scholarly paradigms.

Recommendations

On the basis of my conversations with numbers of administrators, students, and especially faculty, it is apparent to me that in some quarters, and particularly with respect to certain disciplines, any hint of reform meets with at least some vehement indignation and resistance. Both reactions are predicated on the supposition that reform means a lowering of standards. According to some faculty and other graduate alumni, this supposed lessening of rigor and, as a consequence, the shortening of time-to-degree are but crass attempts to compete for students in a tight postbaccalaureate market. In truth, there is justifiable cause for Ph.D. programs to want to compete better with the learned professions and business schools for the best and brightest graduating seniors. Reform is not, however, for the purpose of making a Ph.D. easier to acquire. The purpose is to make doctoral education more appealing in order to attract students who not only persevere, regardless of the drudgery and transferential relationships with faculty mentors, but also are among the most intellectually gifted and imaginative. Many of these potentially outstanding doctoral students opt for the law, business administration, or even medical school because these professional degree programs are at least close-ended. Doctoral study, principally because of the dissertation, is open-ended. In other words, the limited appeal of doctoral study concerns not just the time it typically takes to complete the Ph.D., although this is certainly a consideration in some humanities and social sciences disciplines, but also the disconnectedness of the postqualifying examination period.

The policy statement of the Association of American Universities and the Association of Graduate Schools (1990) speaks directly to the need to reduce time-to-degree and train more U.S.-born students to meet the forecasted increases in demand for faculty members (see, for example, Bowen and Sosa, 1989). And CGS (1991b, p. 1) quotes from a document prepared by the University of Michigan that "there is the need in many fields to expedite progress through the dissertation process without adversely affecting the quality of the experience of the research itself." With a firmly established sense that the quality of doctoral education should not and need not be compromised by reform, I offer the following recommendations that gloss, underscore, and expand on several of the recommendations listed in the reports and studies cited in this chapter.

Recommendations to Faculty. First, *tie at least some coursework to possible dissertation topics.* I have already alluded to the widely held belief among deans, faculty, and students that the dissertation is less of a problem in the sciences than it is in the humanities. While not asking why the humanities cannot be more like the sciences, we should strongly endorse the imperative, expressed in CGS (1991b), of tying some coursework to possible dissertation topics. Faculty should encourage entry-level doctoral students, and even those who may be contemplating a terminal master's, to start narrowing down possible fields of research with the dissertation in mind. The adviser or the director of graduate studies should persist in requiring students to identify and discuss possible dissertation topics.

Second, *limit the length of dissertations.* Some have inveighed against dissertations of excessive length (see Ziolkowski, 1990, pp. 190–191, on average dissertation length by discipline). For fields in which long dissertations are common, theses with as few as seventy to one hundred pages should be encouraged, with an upper limit of two hundred pages imposed. In many cases, it is useful for dissertation writers to present a detailed review of the literature and include exhaustive references and documentation. In the interest of reducing the size of the dissertation and, as a consequence, the writing time, students could display their capacity to engage in scholarly documentation and their familiarity with the literature in term papers submitted prior to, or as a part of, the qualifying examinations.

Third, *allow collaboration and innovative approaches.* In line with CGS's

(1991b) recommendations on the dissertation as a report of scholarship, I propose not only that there be greater flexibility and latitude to allow for collaborative efforts (including co-authored dissertations and the inclusion of published or publishable materials) but also that advisers and defense committees permit the use of innovative approaches, such as autobiography, as long as an acceptable equivalent of traditional scholarly rigor is maintained.

Recommendations to Administrators. First, *hold faculty accountable for student progress*. The important adviser-advisee relationship suggests that faculty should be held accountable for students' timely progress toward the degree—specifically, toward completion of the dissertation. Deadlines should apply to faculty as well as to students. Faculty should hold students to an overall period devoted to the dissertation of no more than two years, with strong encouragement to finish in a year. As already occurs at some universities, faculty should be awarded or censured on the basis of how they carry out their responsibilities to students. For instance, faculty who do not return dissertation chapters in a timely fashion deserve to be penalized in some formal manner for their delinquence.

Second, *establish accountability procedures*. Because some faculty will claim that their academic freedom stands to be violated at the slightest hint of any administrative meddling in the relationship between themselves and their advisees, chief academic officers, as well as graduate deans, faculty councils, and department chairs, need to establish and implement strict accountability policies and procedures. Just as faculty are increasingly being held accountable for effective teaching, they should also submit to scrutiny with respect to their dissertation advisees' progress.

Conclusion

The foregoing recommendations have as their principal objectives the improvement of the process and eventually the replenishment and strengthening of the professoriate. The quality of the faculty of the next generations is, in large part, a function of how we deliver doctoral education today and in the future. And, ultimately, now and in the future much of the success or failure of doctoral education hangs on the role and nature of the dissertation.

References

Association of American Universities and the Association of Graduate Schools. *Institutional Policies to Improve Doctoral Education*. Washington, D.C.: Association of American Universities and the Association of Graduate Schools, 1990.

Bowen, W. G. *Annual Report of the President. Graduate Education in the Arts and Sciences: Prospects for the Future*. Princeton, N.J.: Princeton University Press, 1981.

Bowen, W. G., and Rudenstine, N. L. *In Pursuit of the Ph.D.* Princeton, N.J.: Princeton University Press, 1992.

Bowen, W. G., and Sosa, J. A. *Prospects for Faculty in the Arts and Sciences.* Princeton, N.J.: Princeton University Press, 1989.

Council of Graduate Schools. *Research Student and Supervisor: An Approach to Good Supervisory Practice.* Washington, D.C.: Council of Graduate Schools, 1991a.

Council of Graduate Schools. *The Role and Nature of the Doctoral Dissertation.* Washington, D.C.: Council of Graduate Schools, 1991b.

Ziolkowski, T. "The Ph.D. Squid." *American Scholar,* 1990, 59 (2), 177–195.

RUSSELL G. HAMILTON is professor of Brazilian and Lusophone African literature and dean of graduate studies and research at Vanderbilt University, Nashville, Tennessee.

Integration of knowledge is as critical to the understanding of our world as the discovery of new knowledge. In fact, the extension of specialization requires new forms of integration. We need scholars who can synthesize, look for new relationships between the parts and the whole, relate the past and the future to the present, and ferret out patterns of meaning that cannot be seen through traditional disciplinary lenses.

Academic Integration: Going Beyond Disciplinary Boundaries

Muriel L. Blaisdell

> Universities tend to see tasks or problems through the lens of their subjects and courses. When an issue cuts across the provinces of departments or professions it requires "interdisciplinary" treatment. But because academic provinces are also political territories, interdisciplinary projects are quickly politicized—and the politics of the academy are legendary, fertile ground for satirists from Aristophanes to Alison Lurie.
> —Donald A. Schön (1987, p. 310)

Rationale for Integration

Reform in American education often occurs piecemeal. Reforms that may profoundly affect one segment of a student's education may have little bearing on another part. Experimentation and reforms in undergraduate education that have been characterized as liberal or general education have not always, perhaps not often, produced corollary changes in courses in majors and in professional or graduate education. Curriculum changes intended to mitigate the negative consequences of undergraduate specialization and to provide more student-centered pedagogies began at Harvard, Columbia, and the University of Chicago in the 1940s and spread throughout the nation with increasing urgency and in shorter cycles as alternatives to technical training and to early disciplinary isolation and professionalization proliferated. As Birnbaum (1986, p. 59) noted, "The experiments at Columbia and Harvard, moreover, were confined to their undergraduate colleges, while their graduate schools (of more influence on American education) allowed the disciplines to run amok." The strong tide toward reform in liberal or general education has taken the institutional form of adjustments in distribution requirements and the addition of multi- and interdisciplinary courses.

Although the variety of interdisciplinary programs is greater at the undergraduate level, interdisciplinary graduate education is currently available in most regions of the country. Programs in environmental sciences, American studies, women's studies, history and philosophy of science, conflict resolution, and other integrated fields create environments for graduate work that combine theory, research, and application of this knowledge. Graduate education also is indirectly affected because teaching assistants may be assigned undergraduate teaching tasks for which their training in narrow disciplinary research ill prepares them. Now is an ideal time for graduate educators to put aside ambivalence about graduate education as college teacher preparation. Graduate students who become capable of disciplinary and interdisciplinary curriculum development, teamwork, and pedagogical innovations will have positive effects on the disciplines. A greater emphasis on teaching can promote awareness of the structure of knowledge in established and emerging disciplines. The growth of interdisciplinary programs in England, continental Europe, and the United States suggests that, gradually, universities are recognizing that there are advantages to pluralism in graduate education and that graduate students can become teaching professionals as well as research professors (Kockelmans, 1979; Newell, 1986).

Interdisciplinary Lexicon

Before going further, it is important to review the terms for various forms of interdisciplinarity. *Discipline,* as defined by Kockelmans (1979, p. 127), is "a branch of learning or a field of study characterized by a body of intersubjectively acceptable knowledge, pertaining to a well-defined realm of entities, systematically established on the basis of generally accepted principles with the help of methodical rules or procedures; for example, mathematics, chemistry, history." Just as disciplines have their subdisciplines, interdisciplinarity also has a variety of forms. A series of terms implies escalating levels of integration and increasingly obligatory reliance on groups and teamwork.

According to Klein (1990), the sequence of terms includes *multi-, pluri-, cross-, inter-,* and *transdisciplinary.* In education today, multidisciplinary education is the typical pattern. The student taking courses in English literature, political science, biology, and Spanish may or may not see connections among these disciplines. In a multidisciplinary system, connections are not explained within each course but depend on whatever integrative efforts the student makes. Pluridisciplinary work occurs in adjacent fields, such as biology and chemistry, in which understanding and competence in one area carry over to another. Crossdisciplinary undertakings are based on the principle that a single discipline is not fully explicable in terms of that discipline alone. For example, the history of science uses methods from the humanities and social sciences to describe or explicate scientific research and discovery. Interdisciplinary efforts require integration of materials or ideas in such a way that different disciplines may be either clearly recognizable or considerably transformed. Transdisciplinary work shares with interdisciplinary work a commitment to integration and is even more likely to be conducted by groups working on a complex social problem. Reflective researchers and scholarly teachers eventually will need to confront the entire "interdisciplinary archipelago" (see Klein, 1990, pp. 40–54).

Multi- and interdisciplinary settings differ in the extent to which integration is attempted and expected. Multidisciplinary projects and courses retain a significant disciplinary form, and integration occurs as managers or students find ways to synthesize and integrate reports, texts, or other materials offered by a variety of disciplinary perspectives. In multidisciplinary programs, each participant retains a strong allegiance to disciplinary traditions while working cooperatively with other participants. There is no necessity in multidisciplinary work for one member of the team to learn methodologies, processes, or skills associated with other disciplines or to rethink his or her own perspective. In a research setting, the effort of integrating the sections is assigned to the project manager; in courses, each student is given the responsibility to integrate the disciplinary components. Faculty members may think that the topics, syllabi, seminars, or lectures provide students with opportunities for integration and, consequently, may underestimate the students' struggles to integrate course materials. Redirection of (student and faculty) minds that have practice in analysis toward synthesis and integration is a complex task. Graduate teaching assistants are often in the position to help students learn new skills, but they are likely to need faculty help to fulfill this goal.

Interdisciplinary work requires greater stamina for interaction among representatives of different disciplines than is characteristic of multidisciplinary work. Moreover, it requires receptivity, flexibility, and new thinking. Interdisciplinarians must construct their work together because a new single conceptual framework using theories, methods, or other tools from several disciplines is being created. Two fields cannot merely be juxtaposed as in the equation Discipline A + Discipline B = Interdiscipline AB; in order to work, the addition A + B must equal the new Discipline C.

Problem of Undisciplined Problems

Contrasting social problems as they are in society with the way in which they are studied in academic settings, Rose (1986) has noted that academic research problems in the social sciences have a tendency to be *esoteric*, reflecting circularly on academic disciplines, whereas governmental or social policy issues are *exoteric*. Exoteric research responds to political and contextual problems, that is, to the kinds of issues that have an interdisciplinary character. For instance, interdisciplinary teamwork has been a significant feature of groups involved in health care, environmental assessment, and technology development. High levels of funding for science, engineering, and health care research seem to promote the evolution of new research areas in departments and graduate and undergraduate education units. Roy (1979) drew two conclusions from his case study of the fields of materials science and geochemistry. First, financial and political incentives have been more important than intellectual factors in changing university organization in the direction of interdisciplinarity. Second, "the best research can only be done in the context of the whole problem" (1979, p. 166). After all, few, if any, of the social problems that we face come within single disciplinary boundaries. As universities become increasingly amenable to exoteric determination of problems, more interdisciplinary researchers and teachers will be needed.

Philosophers of science who study disciplinary development have shown how, historically and institutionally, disciplines have pursued problem solving in such a way as to produce clusters of specialists separated by wide gaps. In much graduate training, specialization within the discipline is guaranteed by an advising process that apportions the specialty of the mentor to graduate students. In contrast, Campbell (1986, p. 30) represents interdisciplinary knowledge as a "fish-scale model of omniscience" in which growth spreads around a center with a zone intersecting adjacent fields.

Pelikan (1983, p. 36) criticized interdisciplinary graduate programs for admitting graduate students on the equation "An M.A. knowledge of one field + an M.A. knowledge of another field = a Ph.D. knowledge of the interrelation between those two fields." While interrelations between two fields constitute one aspect of interdisciplinary education, interdisciplinary work asks students to use conceptual frameworks and integrative thinking to discover solutions to both old and new problems, a task that sometimes requires interdisciplinary specialization. It is imperative that interdisciplinary educators not lose the practical applications of interdisciplinarity in theoretical detail. Materials science, in Roy's (1979) study, solved problems by borrowing from engineering, mathematics, and the physical sciences, especially mechanics and chemistry. Venn-type diagrams of considerable complexity are required to show the field-to-field transfer of knowledge to solve interdisciplinary problems (Klein, 1990, p. 85).

Development of Interdisciplinary Programs

Interdisciplinary programs often emerge when universities recognize the gap between "disciplined research and undisciplined problems" (Rose,

1986, p. 67). Thoughtful interdisciplinarians do not attempt to resuscitate the outdated, "Leonardesque" longing to be a "Renaissance man" who understands all current knowledge (Campbell, 1986, p. 31). Although the history of science abounds with biographies of great synthetic minds who comprehended many disciplines and understood the relationships among them, today many single disciplines contain far more knowledge than a single mind can master. With the proliferation of disciplines, multiple authorship of scientific articles and books has increased. Telephones, fax machines, and electronic mail networks allow researchers to put their minds together around the globe. Although the model of the individual master has been largely replaced by the model of the team, students are often taught the older model of competence and mastery (Roy, 1979). If the isolation model is presented to students as the standard to which they should aspire, they are doomed to disappointment and disillusionment. History shows that disciplines fission as knowledge expands. In contrast to Galileo, physicists today usually do not consider themselves fully competent in all of physics, but only in one or two of its branches. This is not a confession that one is mentally less capable than the seventeenth-century polymath but rather a recognition that knowledge in twentieth-century physics has quantitatively overtaken the capacity of a single mind. It is a false hope to expect interdisciplinary thinking to transcend the limitations of our neural network; however, there are ways that interdisciplinarity can help to solve complex problems by redefining disciplinary domains and by seeking alternatives to individual mastery.

Recently, I was told by several colleagues that the establishment of degree-granting interdisciplinary graduate programs in their universities is still hampered by perceptions and experiences indicating that such degrees are less marketable than those in standard fields. Positions with government agencies and academic jobs are still mainly based on disciplines. Especially in periods of economic retrenchment, conservative responses are common in education institutions. This means that graduate students may need to look beneath the surface of departmental or program names for an interdisciplinary approach to graduate education. For example, interdisciplinarity may find a niche, as it has at Rutgers in New Brunswick, New Jersey, in a human ecology program. This field includes the varied social sciences of anthropology, psychology, sociology, and geography, as well as environmental sciences. The program offers undergraduate degrees in human evolution and in international environmental studies. A Ph.D. student, however, takes a degree from one of the departments that contribute to teaching the human ecology program. Degree-granting interdisciplinary programs can be arranged by individual planning and with interdepartmental agreement. The moral of this story is that a graduate student may seek and find interdisciplinary graduate options, even when degrees are conferred by a single department. Interdisciplinary undergraduate programs may often be indicators that faculty are congenial to interdisciplinary research and dissertations.

Fields such as the history of science have grown out of interdisciplinary energy and with the hybrid vigor that comes from the juxtaposition of the natural and social sciences and the humanities. Gradually, the history of science has been accepted as a kind of subdiscipline within history. The development of the variegated field of science studies demonstrates the concern that scholars have for closer connections between the history, philosophy, sociology, and psychology of science and the literary studies of science writing. The reconfiguration of fields is designed to restore a strong connection to scientific and technological knowledge and research. One example of this rich vision of science and its context is the Science and Technology Studies Program at Virginia Polytechnic Institution and State University at Blacksburg. That program includes the sociology as well as the history and philosophy of science. This unified approach to science and technology prepares students for science advisory posts with government and nongovernment agencies, as well as for professorships.

Interdisciplinary graduate coursework provides students who aspire to be college teachers with opportunities to learn to work across, as well as within, several disciplines. Often graduate education is effectively insulated from the domain of undergraduate education, although the latter is where many (or, in some fields, most) will invest a significant portion of their energy and professional commitment as professors. A shock to the self-esteem and confidence of new faculty is almost a foregone outcome because they are not educated in graduate programs about the kinds of thinking, curriculum development skills, and pedagogies that they will need during their careers as teachers in colleges and universities.

The evolution of disciplines finds expression in the form of the university. As disciplines fission or fuse, the university finds a niche for the mutations that persist. For more than twenty years now disciplinary education has been unable to either describe or promote solutions to complex societal problems. Mixed disciplinary studies programs, such as Women's Studies, African American Studies, Peace Studies, and Latin American Studies, have been significant and standard parts of the academic landscape; nonetheless, the formation of new institutional forms has often been superficial, and the cooperation among disciplines has been made more difficult by the university's conservative disciplinary style. Interdisciplinary work is not merely cooperation among disciplines. It is integrative work, based on the building of inclusive conceptual frameworks, not just different containers in which old disciplines may more congenially jostle each other. New ethnic and area studies encouraging cooperation among faculty with different academic backgrounds are clearly a necessary condition, even though the project of fully developing the theory and epistemology of interdisciplinarity is still a work in progress.

Interdisciplinary Distinction

Interdisciplinarity is rightly associated with activities that call on, draw from, or contribute to a variety of subject fields, but it is not appropriate to use the word *generalist* as a synonym for *interdisciplinarian*. Some interdisciplinary studies are general and broad, but many are quite specific, as they are in marine ecology or materials science. When used in connection with knowledge, the words *general* and *broad* imply that knowledge grows continuously larger through expansion, like a balloon being blown up. As the volume of knowledge enlarges, teaching follows through correspondingly massive coverage of the factual and conceptual content of the discipline. In this figure of speech, one who learns several disciplines or pursues an interdisciplinary course of study is stretched, perhaps to the point of bursting. Unless a new language is devised that accurately emphasizes the uniqueness of interdisciplinary education, it is likely that interdisciplinary work will be described by those outside the paradigm as watered-down versions of disciplinary courses. Interdisciplinary scholarship is best understood to involve selection, consolidation, and integration of disciplinary and conceptual materials. Interdisciplinary courses or research follow the contours of the problem being studied through and among disciplines.

Interdisciplinary Cooperation

One can frequently hear the plaintive cry of a professor who teaches a survey course of a discipline such as sociology, or even a subdiscipline such as American history: "I can't cover this subject in a fifteen-week semester (or a ten-week quarter or a year-long course)." Certainly, complete coverage is an impossible task that is made manageable by abstracting what the professor and peers deem to be highlights, the most interesting or pertinent points. Another significant goal of interdisciplinary, integrative teaching and learning is the process of creating a framework for a paradigmatic understanding of the structure of a discipline, when no understanding is really complete. "The myth of unidisciplinary competence," as Campbell (1986, p. 32) calls it, is a dangerous, though common, belief in academia. Even in single disciplines, comprehensive competence is characteristic of groups, not of individuals, who have all they can do to understand one subspecialty with some degree of competence and integrity. Newer disciplines and interdisciplinary areas are ideally situated to be more honest by being less arrogant in their claims of individual mastery. Isaac Newton's famous line in a letter to Robert Hooke, "If I have seen further it is by standing on the shoulders of giants," may have been a facetious comment for Newton, but it is literally true for us. The key difference is that we have to substitute the plural pronoun *we* for Newton's *I*. The social construction and collectivity of knowledge is an important part of the conceptual reformation of graduate education and its relationship to scholarship.

Histories of academic disciplines are instructive for those who aspire to teach and conduct research in these fields, because a sociological approach to knowledge helps to explain the difference between logic and experience. The discipline of anthropology, for example, contains "congeries of subdisciplines . . . a hodgepodge of all novelties that struck the scholarly tourist's eye when venturing into exotic lands—a hodgepodge of skin color, physical stature, agricultural practices, weapons, religious beliefs, kinship systems, language, history, archaeology, and paleontology" (Campbell, 1986, p. 33). Students infrequently learn adequately how departments retain unified exteriors while containing eclectic and fragmented interiors. Departments may be easily mistaken for single disciplines, although lacking unifying paradigms or principles. Indeed, there is often unrealized potential within single departments such as anthropology and geography for authentic interdisciplinary education. The university, its disciplines and its divisions show how much we have inherited from Greek, Roman, Italian, British, and German scholarly traditions. As Swoboda (1979, p. 59) stated succinctly, "From France . . . came the *Ecole Polytechnique;* from Germany, the modern university." Industrialization and the scientific and empirical traditions of Europe altered substantively the academic world that we inhabit. Empirical and positivist traditions that came into American colleges and universities in the nineteenth and early twentieth centuries are still deeply entrenched in disciplinary and departmental structures. A graduate student who understands the process of mutation of disciplines is probably better equipped to invent alternatives to the disciplinary tradition.

Recommendations

Both the Carnegie Foundation (Boyer, 1990) and Rice (1991) have raised the hope of unifying the scholarship of teaching and integration through a valuing of the concrete, connected knowing of scholars who are both teachers and researchers. Inspired by the ideal of democratic community, Boyer (1990, p. 74) has expressed hope of bringing the theory and practice of new scholars and teachers into an integrated community: "It is our conviction that if scholarship is to be redefined, graduate study must be broadened, encompassing not only research, but integration, application, and teaching. It is this vision that will assure . . . a new generation of scholars, one that is more intellectually vibrant and more responsive to society's shifting needs." Interdisciplinary education can facilitate the preparation of college professors in many areas.

    Recommendations to Faculty. First, *practice developing group projects, papers, and presentations using several disciplines.* The teacher-scholar asks, "How can my classroom behavior, my relationships to students, colleagues, curriculum, assignments, and evaluation, reflect my goal to teach in an integrative and interdisciplinary way?" Interdisciplinarians are more likely than others to teach in teams and to need an understanding of team-building and cooperative methodologies. Cooperative interactions and congenial differences may come as a positive surprise to students who have witnessed competition and turf battles among their professors over intellectual territory. Practical manifestations of interdisciplinary work include promotion of communication skills, shared leadership, and conflict resolution (Campbell, 1986). An interdisciplinary teacher must not be ethnocentric about single perspectives and must resist xenophobic reactions to new subject fields. (With so much to learn in the world, perhaps it is more a failure than a success when a graduate student enters the same subfield as that of his or her adviser!)

Cooperative work is often a strain for scholars who are adapted to a hierarchical and authoritarian system. Group tasks almost always involve some degree of uncertainty and ambiguity that must be resolved (Taylor, 1986). Belenky, Clinchy, Goldberger, and Tarule (1986, p. 277) urge connected teaching practices that can be expressed in interdisciplinary course construction as well as in the pedagogy with which the course is conducted: "A connected teacher is not just another student; the role carries special responsibilities. It does not entail power over the students; however, it does carry authority, an authority based not on subordination but on cooperation." Interdisciplinary pedagogy is an alternative to, and critique of, hierarchical and chain-of-command styles in teaching, advising, and learning.

Interdisciplinary faculty members need to plan on a lifetime of self-initiated faculty development in new subject areas and in new pedagogical techniques in order to involve students effectively and creatively. In programs such as the School of Interdisciplinary Studies at Miami University, faculty regularly establish new team-teaching partnerships. Faculty members have widely varied educational backgrounds, including American history, botany, psychology, American studies, paleontology, economics, geochemistry, rhetoric and composition, design, ecology, intellectual history, theater and performance studies, political science, and geography. My own areas of knowledge in the history, philosophy, and social studies of science have sometimes, but not nearly always, been featured in the courses that we have created. More often than not, each of us must add new topics and techniques to our teaching repertoires. Interdisciplinary teaching provides continual faculty development and renewal for professors many years beyond graduate study. "What a university should promote . . . is the ability to acquire skills continually throughout a working lifetime and an understanding of the way in which such skills can be applied to solving problems" (Prange, Jowett, and Fogel, 1982, p. 103). The focus on changing skills is particularly vital when professionals commonly change fields several times during their careers.

Second, *do not limit the permutations and combinations of fields for interdisciplinary courses.* There is virtually no limit to the permutations and combinations of fields that work well in interdisciplinary courses. Courses can be effective when the disciplines have much in common, for example, biology and geology, or when they are very distinct, as with biology and philosophy. Courses that take advantage of pluridisciplinary carryover from adjacent fields are often convenient ways to introduce students to interdisciplinary thinking. At Miami University, student needs motivated our discovery of pluridisciplinary qualities where we had not recognized them before. When student assessment data indicated that our graduates lacked quantitative knowledge and skills, we established a program of quantitative reasoning across the curriculum. In doing so, we found more quantitative work in humanities disciplines than we had expected. Writing-across-the-curriculum programs have also given students a chance to use skills and concepts developed in the humanities in social and natural science settings.

In most interdisciplinary teaching, exploration of the relationships among various disciplines should be an explicit part of the course. In a course involving biology and medical ethics at Miami University, for example, we structure our activities on the model of the interdisciplinary medical care team and hold case conferences to help students learn to integrate materials from human biology, ethical reasoning, and psychosocial issues, and to use these materials to draw conclusions that are reasonable scientifically, ethically, and socially. Students write synthetic papers, organize panels, and give presentations with the whole seminar participating. The effectiveness of this course is enhanced because students can identify ways to use the course material in their lives.

The interdisciplinary course may, indeed, be quite general or very narrowly focused; it may use either closely allied or disparate subject material; it may be introductory or advanced; and it may be taught alone or with others. What makes a course interdisciplinary is the commitment to continual integration and the recognition that no one can ever be like Leonardo da Vinci!

Third, *involve students*. Student involvement in interdisciplinary education is essential since integration is an active process that is often new to students. Students generally respond favorably to the interactive features of cooperative group work. Sometimes they come to see unintegrated learning as resembling "paint-by-numbers" exercises, in which one must stand back and hope that a unified image appears. Pedagogies designed to bring students into the process of learning, teaching, and evaluating their own learning help students gain confidence in themselves as capable integrative learners. As they integrate their coursework in a holistic way, the paint-by-numbers effect diminishes. Illustrating this outcome, assessment studies have shown that students who participate in interdisciplinary programs have the following qualities: greater sensitivity to ethical issues, greater ability to synthesize or integrate, greater awareness of public issues, more creative or unconventional thinking, more humility and listening skills, and greater sensitivity to assumptions and biases (Newell, 1990).

Students in interdisciplinary education have the opportunity to interact with their teachers as co-learners. One of the best features of integrative teaching techniques is the way in which it promotes discovery learning for both the student and the faculty member. When projects are not cookbook exercises but rather authentic integrative explorations, students and teachers have opportunities for equitable relationships and even for role reversals. As a co-learner rather than an expert, the faculty member can share his or her own writings or data with students in a nonauthoritarian way. Students often learn more when they share the teaching functions as individuals or in groups. Group work is particularly consistent with interdisciplinary studies, and the dynamics of groups (especially of small groups) is an important aspect of interdisciplinary classrooms. Words such as *facilitator, coordinator, co-learner, collaborator,* and *catalyst* may describe the interdisciplinary teacher's relationships to students better than the more orthodox terms such as *expert, authority,* and *master learner.* As cooperation replaces competition, assessment modes such as the student portfolio may supplement or replace standard examinations.

Recommendation to Administrators. The sole recommendation here is to *make integration easier.* Colleges or universities can either greatly help or successfully strangle interdisciplinary graduate programs. There are several problems that pioneering programs have managed to overcome:

- Easing administrative barriers to cross-listed courses
- Finding equitable means to share the revenue raised by team-taught courses
- Acknowledging that team teaching requires such extensive consultation within the interdisciplinary team that it equals or exceeds the work needed to prepare an individually taught disciplinary course
- Recognizing through assessment and academic credit the interdisciplinarity of life experiences
- Permitting students broad options in choosing interdepartmental graduate committees
- Nurturing faculty development via grants for interdisciplinary course development by individuals and groups and for fellowship study in new fields, and supporting conference travel to learn about new fields, pedagogies, and teaching technologies
- Offering courses with integrative goals specifically for graduate students (as well as for undergraduates)
- Including interdisciplinarians on grant committees
- Redirecting institutional rewards to encourage curriculum and pedagogical innovation and risk taking

- Providing workshops and in-service programs on team building, small group work, active and cooperative learning, portfolio assessment, and conflict resolution.

Conclusion

The ideal of holistic knowledge can be realized in a more complete way when there is less separation between fields of discourse, faculty and students, and institutions and people. *Integration* is a word commonly associated with racial desegregation and the struggle for civil liberties and equality. Desegregation of our society remains a complex and incomplete task. The desegregation of the curriculum also has many layers and levels. The work of philosophers, historians, and social scientists has begun to disclose how knowledge is discovered and rediscovered. Among the intellectual adventures ahead for the new scholar is the opportunity to carry forward the effort of desegregating and integrating our curricula and our thinking. Just as in the case of meaningful integration among people of different heritages, if one group establishes all of the rules and dominates all other groups, what results is not integration but assimilation. Similarly, integration in education must be characterized by a cooperative effort to create something new, while continuing to appreciate the integrity of the separate components.

References

Belenky, M. F., Clinchy, B. M., Goldberger, N. R., and Tarule, J. M. *Women's Ways of Knowing: The Development of Self, Voice, and Mind.* New York: Basic Books, 1986.

Birnbaum, N. "The Arbitrary Disciplines." In D. E. Chubin, A. L. Porter, F. A. Rossini, and T. Connolly (eds.), *Interdisciplinary Analysis and Research: Theory and Practice of Problem-Focused Research and Development.* Mt. Airy, Md.: Lomond, 1986.

Boyer, E. L. *Scholarship Reconsidered: Priorities of the Professoriate.* Princeton, N.J.: Princeton University Press, 1990.

Campbell, D. T. "Ethnocentrism of Disciplines and the Fish-Scale Model of Omniscience." In D. E. Chubin, A. L. Porter, F. A. Rossini, and T. Connolly (eds.), *Interdisciplinary Analysis and Research: Theory and Practice of Problem-Focused Research and Development.* Mt. Airy, Md.: Lomond, 1986.

Klein, J. T. *Interdisciplinarity: History, Theory, and Practice.* Detroit: Wayne State University Press, 1990.

Kockelmans, J. J. "Why Interdisciplinarity?" In J. J. Kockelmans (ed.), *Interdisciplinarity and Higher Education.* University Park: Pennsylvania State University Press, 1979.

Newell, W. H. *Interdisciplinary Undergraduate Programs: A Directory.* Oxford, Ohio: Association for Integrtative Studies, 1986.

Newell, W. H. "Interdisciplinary Curriculum Development." In W. G. Doty and J. T. Klein (eds.), *Issues in Integrative Studies.* Special Number: Interdisciplinary Resources No. 8. Oxford, Ohio: Association for Integrative Studies, 1990.

Pelikan, J. *Scholarship and Its Survival: Questions on the Idea of Graduate Education.* Princeton, N.J.: Princeton University Press, 1983.

Prange, W. W., Jowett, D., and Fogel, B. *Tomorrow's Universities: A Worldwide Look at Educational Change.* Boulder, Colo.: Westview Press, 1982.

Rice, R. E. "The New American Scholar: Scholarship and the Purposes of the University." *Metropolitan Universities,* 1991, *1* (4), 7–18.

Rose, R. "Disciplined Research and Undisciplined Problems." In D. E. Chubin, A. L. Porter, F. A. Rossini, and T. Connolly (eds.), *Interdisciplinary Analysis and Research: Theory and Practice of Problem-Focused Research and Development.* Mt. Airy, Md.: Lomond, 1986.

Roy, R. "Interdisciplinary Science on Campus. The Elusive Dream." In J. J. Kockelmans (ed.), *Interdisciplinarity and Higher Education.* University Park: Pennsylvania State University Press, 1979.

Schön, D. A. *Educating the Reflective Practitioner: Toward a New Design for Teaching and Learning in the Professions.* San Francisco: Jossey-Bass, 1987.

Swoboda, W. W. "Disciplines and Interdisciplinarity: A Historical Perspective." In J. J. Kockelmans (ed.), *Interdisciplinarity and Higher Education.* University Park: Pennsylvania State University Press, 1979.

Taylor, J. B. "Building an Interdisciplinary Team." In D. E. Chubin, A. L. Porter, F. A. Rossini, and T. Connolly (eds.), *Interdisciplinary Analysis and Research: Theory and Practice of Problem-Focused Research and Development.* Mt. Airy, Md.: Lomond, 1986.

MURIEL L. BLAISDELL is associate professor of interdisciplinary studies at Miami University, Oxford, Ohio. She was a Lilly Fellow and now coordinates the Miami University Senior Faculty Teaching Excellence Program.

*In the academic profession today, there is a disturbing gap between
what is valued as scholarship and the pragmatic needs of the larger
world. In the dominant view of scholarship, research and theory stand
in hierarchically superior relation to practice. An alternative view
suggests that in many fields, knowledge emerges from the
complexity and rigors of practice.*

Scholarly Work and
Professional Practice

R. Eugene Rice, Laurie Richlin

In celebrating the leadership of William Rainey Harper at the new University
of Chicago in 1906, Lyman Abbott articulated what he believed to be the
national characters of scholarship. Scholarship, he observed, was regarded
by the British as "a means and measure of self-development," by the
Germans as "an end in itself," but by Americans as "equipment for service"
(Rudolph, 1962, p. 356). The English and American colonial colleges
needed faculty with the capacity for scholarly integration—the bringing
together of mind and spirit, self and world. The German universities were
more committed to the discovery of knowledge, to the advancement of what
was known. Both the British and German forms of scholarly work are highly
reflective, encompassing the rich contemplative traditions on which they
were built. A third form of scholarly work, the more distinctly American,
moves toward active practice, engagement with the world. It is this kind of
scholarship, by scholars whose work begins with practice, who learn from
lived experience, and who are committed to service, that ought to drive our
professional schools. Unfortunately, this is not always the case.

Normative for almost all professionally oriented programs are the
assumptions that learning precedes doing and that practice is the application of theory. As the professional school has become more firmly ensconced
in the research university, scholarship in practice-related fields has become
subject to the same centripetal pressures toward narrow research as found
in the arts and sciences. In fact, the more prestigious the university, the more
the programs have become concerned with research and scholarship in the
narrowest sense than with, as Jencks and Riesman (1977, p. 252) put it, the
"practical view of what their students need to know."

NEW DIRECTIONS FOR TEACHING AND LEARNING, no. 54, Summer 1993 © Jossey-Bass Publishers

Today, the divergence between theory and practice and between professional preparation and the practical problems in the workplace continues to plague professional schools. This systemic split results in the expression of mixed messages about the kind of scholarship required of students receiving graduate degrees in the professions, especially those students who intend to enter the professoriate rather than professional practice. Graduate education for the professoriate in professional schools must recognize and encourage the applied, and the learning from practice, as well as more traditional forms of scholarly work. Currently, students in professional schools who intend to enter the professoriate face more than the necessary demands of traditional research (and often of teaching and service): In addition, their education must incorporate professional practice. In defining the appropriate types of scholarship for professional school students, we must focus on how professional practice and theory are related. Although graduate students in most programs usually are required to complete a doctorate at a research university before becoming faculty, they may or may not have ever practiced in the field. In some fields (for example, medicine and architecture), ongoing practice is intrinsic to the faculty member's intellectual life; in other fields (for example, education, nursing, and pharmacy), faculty members teach but are usually not expected to practice a profession (Dinham, 1987).

The question that must be asked regarding professional identity and professional preparation is, How much should the nature of education be determined by practitioners? The choice is whether education for the professions should be dominated by abstract consideration of a field's theories or should be focused on training students in the skills necessary to practice their professions in the real world. For graduate students interested in becoming faculty, the decision is between creating theory that could, eventually, inform application or observing the impact of current practice on clients or patients in order for practice to inform theory.

Graduate education that is focused on practice becomes problematic when the faculty are themselves educated as researchers rather than as practitioners, and when the academic reward system demands more abstract than applied work from them. A mismatch occurs between the needs of the professor, given the dominant scholarly norms, and the needs of the student. The bias of the professor is to recreate the researcher, rather than to educate the up-to-date practitioner.

Roots of a Practical Anomaly

One of the great anomalies in the contemporary world of scholarship is that the application of knowledge is systematically devalued in the nation's universities and colleges (and, particularly, among scholars themselves), because the scholarship of practice is the most distinctly American form of academic work. The great land grant institutions were established during the nineteenth century precisely for the purpose of applying knowledge to the enormous agricultural and technical problems confronting society. These schools and their utilitarian missions matched the mood and needs of an emerging nation. This anomaly has multiple roots, but one important strand can be traced back to the emergence of professional education and, specifically, to the impact of Flexner's (1910) report on medical education, an early study of the Carnegie Foundation for the Advancement of Teaching.

Medicine. The Flexner Report revolutionized medical education. Schools of medicine were moved into the research universities, and the scientific component was greatly increased. Two years of study in the basic sciences were prescribed as the necessary foundation for later clinical training. The medical school curriculum was separated into two disjunctive stages—the preclinical and the clinical—reflecting the division between theory and research, on the one hand, and practice, on the other. The sciences—anatomy, biochemistry, physiology, pathology, and pharmacology—are still taught in classrooms and laboratories, that is, in formal academic settings; practical training—for instance, internal medicine, pediatrics, and orthopedics—takes place in hospital settings. The significance of structuring the elements of professional knowledge in this hierarchical way was felt not only in medicine but across the professions as well. The Flexner Report established the pattern for medicine, and the other professions attempted to follow medicine's lead.

Dentistry. Gies's (1926) report was to dentistry what Flexner's (1910) report was to medicine. After the Gies Report, dental schools became affiliated with universities, even though through the mid-1960s dental school faculty were drawn from practice settings. In an important discussion of the problem, Albino (1984, p. 509) observed that "the result was that the dental faculty in clinical disciplines had considerable practical experience, but little appreciation for the academic traditions of scholarship and publication." However, "Career advancement in academic dentistry appears to demand success in . . . three areas [teaching, scholarship, and service], but first and foremost in research and scholarship. . . . As a result, many dental faculty believe they face an ethical as well as practical dilemma: they are forced to choose between providing excellent professional preparation for their students or ensuring their own academic careers" (p. 509).

Pharmacy. The moves to upgrade the requirements for entry into pharmacy parallel those in medicine and dentistry. Currently, there is a five-year bachelor of science program that awards the B.S. in pharmacy and a six-year doctoral program that awards the Pharm.D. The American Council on Pharmacy Education has stated its intent to make the six-year doctoral program the only degree that it accredits. However, there is considerable opposition from members of the National Association of Chain Drug Stores who believe that a doctoral program will overtrain pharmacists in community practice while "under-training the people who go into practice at a hospital or other settings" (Blum, 1991, p. A18). Scholarship in pharmacy also is in the process of changing from a hard science orientation to greater focus on clinical care. With the move toward a single doctorate degree, the system is likely to become more like medicine, with separation between basic science and practice.

Law. The history of preparation for a legal career has been remarkably similar to the history of preparation for the medical profession. In addition to passing a bar examination, requirements moved from apprenticeship alone to apprenticeship *or* law school, to law school *only,* to a law school approved by the American Bar Association (ABA) after a college education. Stevens (1983, p. 113) has reported that "the Flexner Report may have been galling to the ABA, but, because of this indignation and the report's success, it also deeply impressed the association. Three years after the Flexner Report was published, the ABA decided enough was enough, and the members of the Committee on Legal Education and Admissions to the Bar announced that it was 'most anxious to have a similar investigation made by the Carnegie Foundation into the conditions under which the work of legal education is carried on in this country.' "

The result was Reed's (1921) report on legal education. However, Reed's recommendations did not lead to a scientific consensus among legal scholars but instead left the field in a state of "increasing conflict, contradiction, and confusion" (Kimball, 1988, p. 465). As a result, neither the ABA nor legal educators endorsed the Reed Report. And the attempt to make law appear to be as scientific as medicine resulted in the "massive case of intellectual schizophrenia" (Stevens, 1983, p. 264) found today in legal scholarship.

Engineering. In response to the call for scientific research, the field of engineering divided into two components: engineering (which is really engineering science) and engineering technology. In the rush toward science following the launching of Sputnik, major engineering programs began to focus more on conceptual and theoretical aspects (including design theories) than on practice. In response, a separate four-year technology degree was developed by faculty whose real interest was in engineering practice. The Accreditation Board for Engineering and Technology established different criteria for accreditation of the two subfields, and for over twenty-five years the two have functioned separately.

Partly in response to industry's needs and partly due to the shrinking number of engineering students, engineering (science) programs have begun to close the gap between engineering technology programs and themselves by reemphasizing practical rather than theoretical design content in the curriculum. Many academic and professional leaders are calling for a realignment of programs under an overarching engineering accreditation, with the technology programs relabeled as *applied engineering*. If engineering does move back to a single type of program, the diversely prepared faculty in the technical programs will once again be confronted with the need to demonstrate the scholarship of application.

Architecture. In many ways, architecture has faced the same problems as engineering, with a tension between theoretical, design aspects of the field and practical considerations of the real world. As in engineering, the movement of architecture schools to the universities was particularly difficult because "their subject matter traditionally dealt with practical knowledge, not abstract principles or empirical research" (Brown and Gelernter, 1989, p. 62). The growing number of architecture doctoral programs is thought to pose a threat to this pragmatic thrust because the new faculty will be selected with a "research orientation rather than with substantial professional experience and qualifications" (Steward, 1988, p. 10). The dilemma of appropriate education for the field's mission remains, both in curriculum and scholarship, how to "accommodate a profession that values design education, yet wants more technical and practice-oriented instruction" (Fisher, 1989, p. 17).

Nursing. Graduate nursing programs were originally organized to prepare nursing faculty and were often found in departments of education. It was not until the 1960s that master's programs were revised to focus on practice (Glazer, 1986). As a result, "faculties of nursing . . . bear responsibility for the whole range of intellectual endeavor, from basic research to testing-in-practice, to serving and training nurses in the field. While the traditional academic disciplines are concerned almost exclusively with developing knowledge, nursing as an applied field must also be concerned with the attitudes and skills necessary for genuinely professional practice" (Newell, 1989, p. 73). Unlike physicians, nurses usually do not continue to practice when they become faculty. The focus has been on the application of nursing theory to client care, rather than on purely theoretical aspects of nursing.

Education. Glazer (1986) found that the identity of graduate schools of education was more ambiguous than that of professional schools such as medicine, law, and business. The main function of schools of education has been to train and credential kindergarten through high school teachers. Based on his major survey of schools of education, Goodlad (1990, p. 177) reported that emphasis on research "leaped forward for many public universities with each transition in classification—from normal school, to teachers' college, to regional college, to regional university." One general response, primarily by major private universities, has been to retain a school of education while going "out of (or almost out of) the teacher education business" (p. 173). Recently, schools of education in research universities have been called on to learn from the wisdom of practice, to get faculty into the nation's schools and to focus on the student as client. In particular, more credence is being given to learning from interactions in the classroom and with students who learn in different ways.

More Inclusive Context

Graduate educators in the professions are beginning to challenge the hierarchical conception of scholarship that makes application of knowledge derivative and, consequently, second best. One way in which pragmatic scholarship has been developed is through the innovative teaching strategy of case method adopted by business schools. This combination of real-life practice with theoretical consideration has led to a practicum-based curriculum for the students and an application-based scholarship by the faculty. As a result, the ties between faculty research interests and student preparation for practice have been strengthened.

In architecture, as in business, one of the ways in which scholarship has remained useful to professional education has been through workshops (sometimes called clinics), a teaching method that introduces the student to the task of becoming a reflective practitioner (Schön, 1983, 1987). The process of educating the reflective practitioner is complicated and iterative, requiring patience and trust from both faculty and students (Schön, 1987). Architecture schools have moved to utilize assessment and portfolio methods in design studios, with students actively bringing critical review to their work.

Even in medicine, the connection between basic research and practice is being realigned. Harvard Medical School, following the lead of problem-based programs elsewhere, has instituted a program that attempts to build clinical practice into medical education from the very beginning.

Schools of education, in research universities particularly, are being called on to take practice more seriously. In order to incorporate the wisdom of practice into the teacher preparation process, several states have enacted bills requiring faculty who teach methods classes to spend regular time in school classrooms. Goodlad (1990, p. 181) has noted that "recognizing the work [of school improvement] as fundamental, intellectual, and entirely appropriate for serious faculty engagement is the first step that our institutions of higher education must take."

Recommendations

Graduate education must give increased attention to the scholarship of application. Future faculty, as well as future practitioners, are going to need experience in, and understanding of, the world beyond the campus.

Recommendations to Faculty. First, *inform scholarship with the wisdom of practice*. Knowledge is generated from the complexity and demands of practice. Experience is a source of learning and understanding. The wisdom of practice needs to inform and enrich theory. Theory and practice need to be mutually interactive, each building on the other.

Second, *encourage graduate students to inform their scholarship with the wisdom of practice.* Graduate school is often viewed as a time for withdrawal and reflection. The problem is that for many doctoral students this period is not seen as a temporary respite but rather a pattern for life. The current pattern of uninterrupted study from kindergarten to one's first academic appointment is hardly conducive to development of the capacity to apply one's expertise to the complex problems confronting society and to work with students and clients from diverse backgrounds. Following this pattern, faculty run the risk of becoming seriously disconnected from the social reality that they are striving to help their students understand and address. For the necessary interchange to take place, internships, cooperative education placements, or other forms of practical experience need to be included in the preparation for the professoriate. A practical interlude in the preparation of future faculty might serve to reconnect the academy to the larger society.

Recommendation to Administrators. The sole recommendation here is to *value applied research in hiring, promotion, and tenure.* A broader conception of scholarship promises to enrich the work of faculty and to make the graduate school preparation of new faculty more challenging. By means of rewards for applied research in hiring, promotion, and tenure decisions, the scholarly capacity of the individual can be enhanced and the faculty member can continue to grow intellectually, while the academic needs of the students and the institution also are served. This enlarged vision of scholarship, if taken seriously, promises to make tomorrow's professoriate more responsive to the shifting scholarly needs of society.

References

Albino, J. E. "Scholarship and Dental Education: New Perspectives for Clinical Faculty." *Journal of Dental Education,* 1984, *48* (9), 509–513.

Blum, D. E. "3 Big Pharmacy Groups Call for New Doctoral Program to Be Adopted as Entry Level Requirement for Profession." *Chronicle of Higher Education,* December 11, 1991, pp. A15, A18.

Brown, G., and Gelernter, M. "Education: Veering from Practice." *Progressive Architecture,* 1989, *3,* 61–62, 64, 66–67.

Dinham, S. M. "Between Academe and Professional Practice: Initial Reflections on Analyzing the Role of Professional Practice in Higher Education." Paper presented at the Western regional meeting of the Association of Collegiate Schools of Architecture, Tucson, Arizona, 1987. (ED 289 398)

Fisher, T. "P/A Reader Poll Education." *Progressive Architecture,* 1989, *2,* 15–17.

Flexner, A. *Medical Education in the United States and Canada.* Carnegie Foundation for the Advancement of Teaching Bulletin No. 4. Princeton, N.J.: Carnegie Foundation for the Advancement of Teaching, 1910.

Gies, W. J. *Dental Education in the United States and Canada: A Report to the Carnegie Foundation for the Advancement of Teaching.* Bulletin No. 19. Princeton, N.J.: Carnegie Foundation for the Advancement of Teaching, 1926.

Glazer, J. S. *The Master's Degree: Tradition, Diversity, Innovation.* ASHE-ERIC Higher Education Reports, no. 6. Washington, D.C.: Association for the Study of Higher Education, 1986.

Goodlad, J. I. *Teachers for Our Nation's Schools.* San Francisco: Jossey-Bass, 1990.

Jencks, C., and Riesman, D. *The Academic Revolution.* (2nd ed.) Chicago: University of Chicago Press, 1977.

Kimball, B. A. "Review Essay." *Journal of Higher Education,* 1988, 59 (4), 456–468.

Newell, L. J. "The Healing Arts and the Liberal Arts in Context." In R. A. Armour and B. S. Fuhrmann (eds.), *Integrating Liberal Learning and Professional Education.* New Directions for Teaching and Learning, no. 40. San Francisco: Jossey-Bass, 1989.

Reed, A. Z. *Training for the Public Profession of Law.* Princeton, N.J.: Carnegie Foundation for the Advancement of Teaching, 1921.

Rudolph, F. *The American College and University: A History.* New York: Vintage Books, 1962.

Schön, D. A. *The Reflective Practitioner: How Professionals Think in Action.* New York: Basic Books, 1983.

Schön, D. A. *Educating the Reflective Practitioner: Toward a New Design for Teaching and Learning in the Professions.* San Francisco: Jossey-Bass, 1987.

Stevens, R. *Law School: Legal Education in America from the 1850s to the 1980s.* Chapel Hill: University of North Carolina Press, 1983.

Steward, W. C. "Influence from Within the Academy upon Architectural Education." Unpublished manuscript, School of Architecture, University of Nebraska, 1988.

R. EUGENE RICE is dean of faculty at Antioch College, Yellow Springs, Ohio, and past senior fellow with the Carnegie Foundation, where he developed the framework of four types of scholarly activity and their relationship to ways of knowing.

LAURIE RICHLIN is interim director of the Office of Research and Evaluation Studies, Antioch College. She is also executive editor of the Journal on Excellence in College Teaching *and director of the Lilly Conference on College Teaching–West.*

In defining teaching as a scholarly activity, we are obligated to educate graduate students as teacher-scholars. A range of developmental models and teaching-learning frameworks already exist, and these are being applied to the training and mentoring of graduate students as future faculty.

Scholarly Teaching: Developmental Stages of Pedagogical Scholarship

Shirley A. Ronkowski

Current interest in broadening the definition of scholarship seems long overdue. As Boyer (1990, p. 16) so aptly has stated, "The time has come to move beyond the tired old 'teaching versus research' debate and give the familiar and honorable term 'scholarship' a broader, more capacious meaning, one that brings legitimacy to the full scope of academic work." Toward this goal, Boyer (1990) and Rice (1991) have developed a cogent model in which they identify four separate but functionally related scholarships: discovery, integration, application, and teaching. Rice has set the categories into Kolb's (1984) two learning style dimensions; how knowledge is perceived (concrete-abstract) and how it is processed (reflective-active). This new approach has generated renewed discussion about the meaning of scholarship and about the ways in which the university community responds or fails to respond to each of these types of scholarly activity. Each scholarly category enumerates various aspects of the work that faculty do, some of which are recognized and rewarded, others of which are expected and desirable but do not carry the prestige and respect that they deserve. Certainly, the scholarship of teaching fits this latter category. If the respect afforded to teaching is to increase, it is necessary to educate the next generation of faculty about teaching as one of the viable scholarships.

Aspects of Scholarly Teaching

Although teaching has been described and defined in countless ways, Rice's (1991) definition is useful in examining the knowledge base required for scholarly teaching. He has identified three important elements of teaching: *synoptic capacity, pedagogical content knowledge,* and *knowledge about student meaning making.* These aspects of scholarly teaching can be loosely defined by noting a few of the higher-level knowledge and skills involved in each:

Synoptic capacity (academic content knowledge)
  Drawing together various areas of an academic discipline
  Placing concepts in the larger context of the discipline
Pedagogical content knowledge
  Knowledge about the interaction between learning processes and academic content
  Expertise in designing examples, analogies, metaphors, simulations, and so forth, to help students integrate new knowledge into their existing schemas
Knowledge about student meaning making
  Recognition of the diversity of student learning characteristics
  Understanding of general learning principles
  Knowledge about stages of student cognition.

These elements do not statically define the scholarship of teaching; rather, they can be used to begin dialogue on the ways in which teaching as scholarship can be viewed. For example, the teaching-learning process can be viewed as a complex interaction among instructor, student, and content. Each element can then be explored in terms of this description. For example, academic content knowledge might be seen to emphasize the importance of acknowledging the context of an academic discipline and how it interacts with the personal contexts of the learners. The teacher-scholar recognizes that these two contexts constitute the teaching-learning environment. Pedagogical content knowledge can be viewed as the confluence between the affective and cognitive domains in effective learning and teaching. The teacher-scholar's ability to attend to both domains facilitates students' ability to integrate new knowledge into their own thinking processes. Knowledge about student meaning making might involve an understanding of the diversity of learner characteristics and styles. Perhaps it is this element of scholarship that provides the background needed to represent knowledge in diverse and creative ways so as to accommodate the variety of ways in which students perceive and process information.

Experienced scholars proficient in these elements of teaching may or may not be able to articulate their scholarship. Yet, articulation is needed if graduate students in training as future faculty are to value teaching as scholarship and if the next generation of faculty is to build on the current scholarship of teaching. It is not difficult to imagine why knowledge about teaching is often tacit. Faculty develop their teaching abilities over years of practice, often by trial and error. Improvement in their teaching is commonly accomplished through 20-20 hindsight, intuition, and years of discovering which practices work best. Such professional development is customarily done in isolation; collegial conversation usually revolves around the scholarship of discovery, not the scholarship of teaching.

When a profession is practiced without reliance on theoretical models and researched principles, the professionals become *bricoleurs,* "do-it-yourselfers" (Hatton, 1989). It is the way in which bricoleurs approach their work that distinguishes them from the true professional, the scholar. Among other traits, bricoleurs use existing tools and techniques to solve problems rather than design new, specific strategies for specific task situations. Bricoleurs use strategies and skills based on previous experience rather than use theory as the foundation for practice. They do not add to their instructional repertoires except by luck or chance, further distinguishing them from scholars, who extend their professional techniques, skills, and materials through the careful use of principles and theoretical frameworks. Few faculty are bricoleurs when practicing their scholarships of integration, discovery, and practice; however with little time left to devote to classes and students, faculty are unfortunately often bricoleurs when it comes to their teaching. Because teaching has not been recognized as a form of scholarship, accompanied by appropriate rewards and resources, faculty have traditionally practiced the teaching profession as bricoleurs and inadvertently transmitted this approach to their graduate students.

Fortunately, there are numerous ways in which teaching as scholarship is being addressed by the academic community. First, articles and lectures are being disseminated to and by faculty on this subject (see, for instance, the *Journal on Excellence in College Teaching*), and it has been a topic at national meetings such as the Lilly Conference on College Teaching and those sponsored by the American Association for Higher Education. Second, on some campuses, the tenure and review processes are being reexamined to give greater value to teaching (Pister, 1991). Third, those faculty who take the scholarship of teaching as seriously as the other scholarships and who delight in the resulting synergy are dynamic role models for their graduate students, who will soon be colleagues. Fourth, many colleges and universities provide financial and technical support for faculty-initiated instructional projects to improve instruction. These projects may use the latest microcomputer and technological advancements and may be assisted by professional developers who work with faculty to base instructional design on learning principles and empirical data (Johnson, Nicholson, and Ronkowski, 1990). Fifth, there is emerging national recognition of the importance of socializing doctoral-level graduate students into the role of college faculty and into the scholarship of teaching (Boyer, 1989).

Development of the Teacher-Scholar

Most college and university faculty begin their teaching careers as graduate student teaching assistants (TAs). As future faculty, it is during this time that they begin to consider teaching either as bricolage or as scholarship. The importance of educating TAs as teacher-scholars is being recognized on campuses across the nation. In 1986, the first national conference on the employment and training of teaching assistants took place. Since then, two more national conferences have been held and a fourth is planned. A large number of session topics at the first conference dealt with how to establish TA training programs and how to handle various administrative issues. An increasing number of topics at subsequent conferences have emphasized teaching skills, instructional strategies, and research into teaching effectiveness practices. This change in emphasis suggests that a large number of campuses have their training programs in place and are moving toward providing more advanced programs that consider the scholarship of teaching as it applies to TA development.

Those involved in these training programs and conferences are aware of the complexities of teaching and know that for TAs these complexities are not learned all at once. As TAs gain in teaching experience, they undergo changes in how they perceive their role, the way in which they view students, the types of concerns that they have, and even the way in which they define teaching and learning. Progression through these changes can be expected in the socialization of individuals into any professional role, and an understanding of this process can provide a framework for educating the teacher-scholar.

There is a growing body of literature describing the socialization process as it applies to TAs. For example, Sprague and Nyquist (1989) suggest three phases in the development of the TA role: senior learners, colleagues in training, and junior colleagues. Although empirical data to further clarify these phases are still being analyzed (Nyquist, Skow, Sprague, and Wulff, 1991), the three designations can be seen to parallel the classic model basic to socialization theory. This theory identifies three general stages that occur during role socialization: separation, transition, and incorporation (Van Gennep, 1960).

Senior learners are described by Sprague and Nyquist as having been selected to the role because of their own ability as students and they are usually closer in perspective to their students than to faculty. They lack expert knowledge of the subject matter, the learning process, and the university system. According to Sprague and Nyquist (1989, p. 44), "To compensate, they are quick to use a single intellectual framework to inform their teaching and to use a single educational model to guide their practice." This is the stage of role socialization in which the individual separates from a former role (student) and begins to adopt a new one (teacher). Much of this stage is spent feeling between roles (Van Gennep, 1960).

The phase in which TAs become colleagues in training exemplifies the second stage of socialization: transition. During this stage, the concentration is on perfecting skills. TAs at this point in their development "become more concerned about their lack of teaching skills. Their confidence as teachers advances . . . the sense of professional identify starts to emerge. . . . They begin to adapt teaching methods to their own personal styles and to figure out unique solutions to novel problems" (Sprague and Nyquist, 1989, p. 44).

TAs in the final phase, junior colleagues, demonstrate the incorporation stage in which individuals define themselves as members of a new status group. Doctoral students begin to view themselves as colleagues with existing faculty in terms of both the scholarship of discovery and the scholarship of teaching.

Similar models of development have been used to guide professional schools of education in sequencing teacher education courses (Fuller, 1969). They have been used to orient student teachers, to specify and sequence teaching competencies, and to provide standards for self and supervisory teacher assessments (Leland and Cohn, 1991). Although various models exist, descriptions of the stages of professional development are very similar. Depending on the model to which one subscribes, there are either three or four stages of professional teacher development (Leland and Cohn, 1991; Fuller, Parsons, and Watkins, 1974). The developmental stages are viewed as hierarchical, yet cyclical (Pataniczek, 1978), and can be briefly described as follows: Stage 1 focuses on *survival* via the development of basic classroom routines and the establishment of the teacher as an authority; Stage 2 involves development of and *mastery of teaching skills and techniques;* Stage 3 focuses on discovering and *meeting student learning needs* with an orientation toward teacher as facilitator; and Stage 4 emphasizes the teacher as mentor with concerns regarding principles of learning, students as individuals, and *teaching and learning as a reciprocal process.*

Similar developmental stages have been found to occur for TAs (Ronkowski, 1989). From a survey of TA concerns, nine categories were identified and distributed into the three stages based on Fuller's concerns model (Fuller and Brown, 1975). Regardless of amount of teaching experience, the majority of TA concerns were at the survival level: adequacy of self as instructor and leader. This preponderance of survival concerns may result from the common practice of assigning TAs to courses that they have not taught before in order to give them a range of course experience. This practice may result in variety but not depth of teaching experience. Because of the cyclical nature of developmental concerns, each time one teaches or assists a new course, survival-level concerns reemerge. As teachers become more experienced in a particular course, time spent satisfying survival-level concerns lessens (Pataniczek, 1978).

Information about TA developmental stages can be put to very practical use. Awareness of concerns at each stage can help faculty sequence content of TA training orientations and seminars. An understanding of the changes inherent to the TA role and to TA concerns can help faculty choose the appropriate supervisory approaches to use with TAs at the various stages of development (Sprague and Nyquist, 1989; Burden, 1982).

Examination of concern categories in terms of specific elements of teaching may be valuable when helping TAs to gain expertise in specific elements of scholarly teaching. Synoptic capacity begins with Stage 1 concerns about knowing the subject matter well enough to present it logically and correctly. In Stage 2, because the major concern is about teaching skills, we would expect TAs to be ready to focus on manipulating course content in ways that promote learning. Among other skills, this would involve organizing specific areas of the discipline in a variety of ways and conceptualizing material from a variety of perspectives. During this stage, TAs gain flexibility with the academic content and in their teaching skills. Finally, with the Stage 3 concern for student learning, TAs would be interested in using their flexibility to meet student learning needs. This concern would also motivate TAs to use the advanced skills of integrating and contextualizing areas of the academic discipline in their teaching.

Pedagogical content knowledge also can be viewed in terms of the concerns model. In Stage 1, TAs are concerned with creating examples to enhance explanations and enliven the class; in Stage 2, the concern is about providing more appropriate and enlightening examples and analogies that fit with and transform the existing schemas of the learners. Finally, in Stage 3, TAs would be expected to begin using metaphors, stories, allusions, and even simulations to capture the imaginations of students and facilitate highly conceptual learning and critical thinking.

Knowledge of student meaning making begins with knowledge about basic student characteristics such as the variation in their academic backgrounds, their fears and abilities, and their expectations of TAs. This foundational knowledge about students is compatible with Stage 1 TA concerns about their own adequacies. In Stage 2, TAs begin to develop teaching skills and strategies based on general principles of teaching and learning. At this stage, TAs would be expected to use a variety of instructional strategies and begin to identify specific teaching skills to address specific course content. Stage 3 concerns about teaching to student learning needs necessitate knowledge about the variety of students' learning styles and knowledge about changes in students' thinking as they mature through the various stages of cognitive development.

The incorporation of Stage 3 knowledge into each of the elements of teaching is no doubt a challenge that endures throughout the teacher-scholar's professional career. This level of scholarship can make and keep teaching challenging. This is the level at which teaching is academically exciting and intellectually enriching. Faculty who are operating at this level are inspirational to their students and to their colleagues. These faculty can make a significant difference in the education of future teacher-scholars.

Recommendations for Faculty and Administrators

The primary implication of this chapter is that becoming a scholarly teacher is an ongoing, thoughtful process. The following recommendations are designed to enable faculty and administrators to nurture the growth of beginning teacher-scholars through programs based on a developmental model and on scholarly literature.

Create Programs for Teacher-Scholars in Training Using Developmental Models. The developmental model is easily applied to existing TA training programs. Although there are a variety of approaches to TA training activities, the types of activities can be clustered into general categories that are fairly common across the nation (Lambert, Syverson, Hutchings, and Tice, 1991). They can also be categorized according to their appropriateness for TAs at the various stages of development.

For the beginning TA, the senior learner, there are campuswide orientation sessions lasting a single day or extending from one to three weeks on some campuses. Special attention is given to the needs of first-year international TAs (ITAs). In many cases, academic departments also have orientation programs specifically for incoming TAs, lasting from a few hours to a few days. Semester-long seminars provide the first-time TA with basic knowledge and skills needed at the survival level. On some campuses, training seminars are conducted by each academic department or by campuswide programs; smaller campuses tend to use the campuswide approach. Customarily, the faculty member to whom the TA is assigned holds regular meetings to discuss the content of the course and of TA sections.

Feedback is valuable for and appropriate to all TAs, but it is no doubt crucial for beginning TAs who have less knowledge about the effectiveness of their teaching. Critical feedback comes from at least four sources: students, peers, faculty supervisors, and personal review of videotaped classes. Student feedback provides important information but usually does not offer suggestions for improvements. Faculty supervisors are important sources of critical feedback on both content and teaching ability. Some faculty take this responsibility lightly, whereas others conscientiously observe TA classrooms and provide specific guidance for the new TA. Some academic departments have programs designed to structure peer feedback. Peers may observe in classrooms or in microteaching situations where TAs take turns presenting class material to an audience of other TAs. Where available, videotape feedback programs provide TAs with an opportunity to view their own classrooms and themselves from the vantage point of their students. All of these sources of feedback can be extremely useful in helping TAs advance through the developmental process. Unfortunately, after the first year of assistant teaching, it is common that the only formal feedback used is student evaluations. Training for second- and third-phase TAs has tended to be sparse and highly informal.

TAs who have advanced to the second and third phases of development, colleagues in training and junior colleagues, are ready for more advanced skills and teaching opportunities. They have enough experience to be asked to give guest lectures. They may be asked to assist faculty in course planning, create as well as grade examinations, and give input into course revisions. For a fairly small number of experienced TAs, service as a peer consultant or master TA provides an opportunity for professional growth. Depending on the campus, the peer consultant may give skill-training workshops, organize departmental training programs, hold ongoing skill seminars, or facilitate video feedback for less experienced TAs. Instructional improvement grants can offer additional opportunities for advanced TAs. Under these programs, TAs can apply directly for funds to develop course materials for their sections or can be named to assist with faculty-initiated instructional grants. Experienced TAs also may be asked to teach courses as the faculty-of-record, as either visiting lecturers or teaching associates. They then conduct their own courses without faculty guidance, often during the summer months. Unfortunately, because few campuses or departments ease the transition from TA to lecturer, new faculty may be surprised at the number of small but important instructional decisions that they must suddenly make. In experiencing a course as the sole instructional leader, a TA must step into another level of scholarly teaching. TAs at Stage 3 are usually confident and knowledgeable about teaching. As first-time teaching associates or visiting lecturers, they find themselves back at the survival level. This opportunity can be thought of as a bridge between the role of TA and that of assistant professor. It also presents a new dimension of socialization involving separation from the TA role, a period of transition, and, finally, a sense of incorporation into the role of course instructor. Just as the TA role must be learned, so must that of instructor.

Whether working with visiting lecturers, teaching associates, or teaching assistants, an important goal is to provide future faculty with information and perspectives that will take them beyond a bricolage approach and into the scholarship of teaching. Because most experienced faculty have not formally studied teaching as an academic discipline, many are reluctant to discuss teaching in an academic way. But the increasing concern about excellence in postsecondary teaching currently being noted by legislators, college administrators, faculty, parents, and students makes now the time for faculty to examine any bricolage approaches toward their own teaching, to initiate scholarly activities to advance their own teaching, and to assist their graduate students in doing likewise.

Use Existing Frameworks. Increasing numbers of faculty and instructional specialists are seeking to improve training programs for graduate student TAs in ways that acknowledge teaching as scholarship and prepare TAs for their current role and their future role as faculty. Existing scholarly knowledge about teaching can be and is being adapted to the postsecondary level and, specifically, to TAs. Theoretical frameworks and models are being taken from academic literature on teaching and adapted by use by TAs. For example, a conceptual framework involving three types of knowledge, developed by educational psychologists, has been used by TAs to guide teaching decisions (Hess, 1991). It also provides a framework for TAs as they select instructional methods and create assignments and examinations. Another model that has been successfully used with TAs highlights the relationship between instructional methods and student behaviors (Sherer, 1991).

Programs for ITAs have a variety of research and frameworks to consider. They can emphasize conceptual understanding of ITA language and pronunciation needs (Costantino, 1987) or concentrate on skills noted in research on cultural communication patterns in the classroom (Bailey, 1982). They can also be informed by research in education (Tanner, 1991) and ITA experiences and perceptions (Bauer, 1991; Ronkowski, 1987).

The scholarship of teaching provides numerous theoretical frameworks that can be used to design the training, supervision, and evaluation of TAs. There is a large body of scholarly literature to guide faculty supervisors in their classroom observation of TAs and in the way in which they choose to discuss feedback on teaching with their TAs (Cogan, 1973; Sergiovanni, 1976). Examples exist in which these theories have been directly applied in work with TAs (Menges and Rando, 1987; Black and Gates, 1991). Video-tape feedback is a special case of instructional feedback on which theory and research also exist (Fuller and Manning, 1973; Perlberg, 1984). Student feedback is examined in light of research on the reliability, validity, and usefulness of student ratings of instructors (Cashin, 1988).

The approach of presenting TAs with teaching and learning theory as the content of TA training programs and using theoretical frameworks to structure these programs provides consistent treatment of teaching as scholarship. All of those involved with the education of future teacher-scholars need to give the same message: Teaching is more than bricolage; it is a form of scholarship. To be effective, this approach needs to be implemented by both campuswide and departmental programs. Scholarly knowledge about teaching and learning can be addressed both in terms of general teaching-learning processes and in terms of considerations specific to each academic discipline.

Focus on the Discipline. Many disciplines have begun to focus on the preparation of their future college and university teachers. The American Sociological Association with its Teaching Resources Center has long been in the forefront of developing discipline-specific materials that examine the teaching of sociology and how specific concepts can best be taught to undergraduate students (Goldsmid and Wilson, 1980; Campbell, Blalock, and McGee, 1985). Tobias (1990) discusses the problems associated with teaching the physical sciences to nonmajors and to students traditionally underrepresented in those sciences. The University of California, Berkeley has instituted a highly successful and often emulated mathematics achievement program for underrepresented students (Fullilove and Treisman, 1990). An increasing number of presentations are being made at professional association meetings on the specifics of teaching in the field. Journals dedicated to discipline-specific teaching include *The Physics Teacher, Engineering Education, Journal of Geology Education, Teaching Political Science, Journal of Economic Education, Teaching History, Teaching Sociology,* and *Teaching of Psychology.*

If TAs are to be socialized as teacher-scholars, they must be exposed to theoretical knowledge about both the content that they teach and the processes by which they teach it. As future faculty, it is crucial that they learn teaching as scholarship in conjunction with the scholarship of discovery, integration, and practice.

References

Bailey, K. "The Classroom Communication Problems of Asian Teaching Assistants." In C. Ward and D. Wren (eds.), *Selected Papers in TESOL.* Vol. 1. Monterey, Calif.: Monterey Institute of International Studies, 1982.

Bauer, G. "Instructional Communication Concerns of International (Non-Native English-Speaking) Teaching Assistants—a Qualitative Analysis." In J. D. Nyquist, R. D. Abbott, D. H. Wulff, and J. Sprague (eds.), *Preparing the Professoriate of Tomorrow to Teach: Selected Readings in TA Training.* Dubuque, Iowa: Kendall/Hunt, 1991.

Black, B., and Gates, B. "Training Mentors to Observe Classes and Give Feedback." Paper presented at the 3rd national conference on Training and Employment of Graduate Teaching Assistants, Austin, Texas, November 1991.

Boyer, E. L. "Preparing Tomorrow's Professoriate." Keynote address at the 2nd national conference on Training and Employment of Teaching Assistants, Seattle, November 1989.

Boyer, E. L. *Scholarship Reconsidered: Priorities of the Professoriate.* Princeton, N.J.: Princeton University Press, 1990.

Burden, P. "Implications of Teacher Career Development: New Roles for Teachers, Administrators, and Professors." Paper presented at the national summer workshop of the Association of Teacher Educators, Slippery Rock, Pennsylvania, August 1982. (ED 223 609)

Campbell, F. L., Blalock, H. M., and McGee, R. (eds.). *Teaching Sociology: The Quest for Excellence.* Chicago: Nelson-Hall, 1985.

Cashin, W. E. *Student Ratings of Teaching: A Summary of the Research.* Idea Paper No. 20. Manhattan: Center for Faculty Evaluation and Development, Kansas State University, 1988.

Cogan, M. *Clinical Supervision.* Boston: Houghton Mifflin, 1973.

Costantino, M. "Intercultural Communication for International Teaching Assistants: Observations on Theory, Pedagogy, and Research." In N. Van Note Chism and S. B. Warner (eds.), *Institutional Responsibilities and Responses in the Employment and Education of Teaching Assistants: Readings from a National Conference.* Columbus: Center for Teaching Excellence, Ohio State University, 1987.

Fuller, F. F. "Concerns of Teachers: A Developmental Conceptualization." *American Educational Research Journal,* 1969, 6 (2), 207–226.

Fuller, F. F., and Brown, O. H. "Becoming a Teacher." In K. Ryan (ed.), *Teacher Education: The Seventy-Fourth Yearbook of the National Society for the Study of Education.* Vol. 2. Chicago: University of Chicago Press, 1975.

Fuller, F. F., and Manning, B. A. "Self-Confrontation Reviewed: A Conceptualization for Video Playback in Teacher Education." *Review of Educational Research,* 1973, 43, 469–528.

Fuller, F. F., Parsons, J. S., and Watkins, J. E. "Concerns of Teachers: Research and Reconceptualization." Paper presented at the annual meeting of the American Educational Research Association, Chicago, April 1974. (ED 091 439)

Fullilove, R. E., and Treisman, U. P. "Mathematics Achievement Among African American Undergraduates at the University of California, Berkeley: An Evaluation of the Mathematics Workshop Program." *Journal of Negro Education,* 1990, *59* (3), 463–478.

Goldsmid, C. A., and Wilson, E. K. *Passing on Sociology: The Teaching of a Discipline.* Washington, D.C.: Teaching Resources Center, American Sociological Association, 1980.

Hatton, E. "Levi-Strauss's Bricolage and Theorizing Teachers' Work." *Anthropology and Education Quarterly,* 1989, *20,* 74–96.

Hess, C. W. "Three Types of Knowledge: A Thinking Frame for Enhancing the TA Experience." In J. D. Nyquist, R. D. Abbott, D. H. Wulff, and J. Sprague (eds.), *Preparing the Professoriate of Tomorrow to Teach: Selected Readings in TA Training.* Dubuque, Iowa: Kendall/Hunt, 1991.

Johnson, R. A., Nicholson, S. J., and Ronkowski, S. A. "Practical Methods for Involving Faculty and Graduate Assistants in Instructional Improvement." In W. E. Cashin (ed.), *Proceedings of the Seventh Annual Conference of Academic Chairpersons: Developing Faculty, Students, and Programs.* Manhattan: National Issues in Education, Kansas State University, 1990.

Kolb, D. A. *Experiential Learning.* Englewood Cliffs, N.J.: Prentice Hall, 1984.

Lambert, L., Syverson, P., Hutchings, P., and Tice, S. L. "1991 Survey of Teaching Assistant Training Programs: An Overview of Current Practices." Paper presented at the 3rd national conference on Training and Employment of Graduate Teaching Assistants, Austin, Texas, November 1991.

Leland, A. O., and Cohn, J. *4 Stages of Teacher Development.* Dubuque, Iowa: Kendall/Hunt, 1991.

Menges, R. J., and Rando, W. C. "Graduate Teaching Assistants' Implicit Theories of Teaching." In N. Van Note Chism and S. B. Warner (eds.), *Institutional Responsibilities and Responses in the Employment and Education of Teaching Assistants: Readings from a National Conference.* Columbus: Center for Teaching Excellence, Ohio State University, 1987.

Nyquist, J. D., Skow, L., Sprague, J., and Wulff, D. "Research on Stages of Teaching Assistant Development." Paper presented at the 3rd national conference on Training and Employment of Graduate Teaching Assistants, Austin, Texas, November 1991.

Pataniczek, D. "A Descriptive Study of the Concerns of First Year Teachers Who Are Graduates of the Secondary Education Pilot Program at Michigan State University." Unpublished doctoral dissertation, School of Education, Michigan State University, 1978.

Perlberg, A. "When Professors Confront Themselves." In O. Zuber-Skerritt (ed.), *Video in Higher Education.* New York: Nichols, 1984.

Pister, K. S. (ed.). *Report of the Universitywide Task Force on Faculty Rewards.* Oakland, Calif.: Office of the President, University of California, 1991.

Rice, R. E. "The New American Scholar: Scholarship and the Purposes of the University." *Metropolitan Universities: An International Forum,* 1991, *1* (4), 7–18.

Ronkowski, S. A. "International and American TAs: Similarities and Differences." In N. Van Note Chism and S. B. Warner (eds.), *Institutional Responsibilities and Responses in the Employment and Education of Teaching Assistants: Readings from a National Conference.* Columbus: Center for Teaching Excellence, Ohio State University, 1987.

Ronkowski, S. A. "Changes in Teaching Assistant Concerns Over Time." Paper presented at the 2nd national conference on the Training and Employment of Teaching Assistants, Seattle, November 1989. (ERIC HE 023 178; ED 315 012; RIE, June 1990)

Sergiovanni, T. J. "Toward a Theory of Clinical Supervision." *Journal of Research and Development in Education,* 1976, *9* (2), 20–29.

Sherer, P. D. "A Framework for TA Training: Methods, Behaviors, Skills, and Student Involvement." In J. D. Nyquist, R. D. Abbott, D. H. Wulff, and J. Sprague (eds.), *Preparing the Professoriate of Tomorrow to Teach: Selected Readings in TA Training.* Dubuque, Iowa: Kendall/Hunt, 1991.

Sprague, J., and Nyquist, J. D. "TA Supervision." In J. D. Nyquist, R. D. Abbott, and D. H. Wulff (eds.), *Teaching Assistant Training in the 1990s.* New Directions for Teaching and Learning, no. 39. San Francisco: Jossey-Bass, 1989.

Tanner, M. "Incorporating Research on Question-Asking into ITA Training." In J. D. Nyquist, R. D. Abbott, D. H. Wulff, and J. Sprague (eds.), *Preparing the Professoriate of Tomorrow to Teach: Selected Readings in TA Training.* Dubuque, Iowa: Kendall/Hunt, 1991.

Tobias, S. *They're Not Dumb, They're Different: Stalking the Second Tier.* Tucson, Ariz.: Research Corporation, 1990.

Van Gennep, A. *The Rites of Passage.* Chicago: University of Chicago Press, 1960.

SHIRLEY A. RONKOWSKI is academic coordinator in the Office of Instructional Consulting, Teaching Assistant Training Program, University of California, Santa Barbara, and assistant professor in the School of Education, California Lutheran University, Thousand Oaks.

The United States is becoming more diverse in many ways, including race, national origin, and language. It is important to bring into the professoriate as wide a range of experience as possible to reflect the increasing diversity of the student population.

Incorporating Diversity into the Professoriate

Trevor L. Chandler

> Today our educational institutions face pressure to revise academic curricula to meet the needs—and the demands—of an increasingly pluralistic society. . . . What is ultimately at stake is the shape of the American future.
> —Arthur M. Schlesinger, Jr. (1991a)

Challenge and Promise of Increasing Diversity

The twenty-first century is upon us, and as we evaluate our readiness to face the challenges that inevitably lie ahead, we find our society lacking in many respects. Enroute to an impressive list of twentieth-century successes, we have managed to lay waste to large areas of the planet on which we live, to pollute the water that we drink and the air that we breathe, to punch gaping holes in the ozone layer that protects us from the sun's ultraviolet rays, and to visit enormous economic hardships on many of the world's peoples by the manner in which we historically have used and distributed the world's natural wealth. While no one country or group of people can be held solely responsible for all of these ills, each country is affected by the human conditions that exist in other countries. Today, the world is smaller than it was when Columbus set sail in 1492 to find India. Technology has brought us closer to both our friends and our enemies, and the possibility of immediate, worldwide scrutiny of our actions has reduced our options with respect to how we relate to others. In such a world, how much we know of and understand our neighbors will determine the quality of our experiences. The great diversity of the world's cultures is both its strength and potential weakness.

NEW DIRECTIONS FOR TEACHING AND LEARNING, no. 54, Summer 1993 © Jossey-Bass Publishers

Education plays a direct and undeniable role in shaping our responses to the stimuli that we encounter in our individual environments. Graduate education in particular provides us with the tools to manipulate the information that we receive to produce new understandings of the familiar and to make critical suppositions about the unknown. Incorporation of diverse populations and information about those populations into our graduate programs, therefore, is essential to the task of structuring graduate education to meet the challenges of the twenty-first century. By increasing the numbers and the knowledge base of groups that share our world, we can make the campus a laboratory where the results of the experiments will have worldwide implications.

But not everyone involved in education agrees on the degree of emphasis that should be placed on ethnic and cultural perspectives (S. Steele, 1990a, 1990b; D'Souza, 1991; Finn, 1990). While there is some agreement on the increasing complexity of the world and the role that ethnic diversity plays in that complexity, there is a tendency to see as divisive and contrary to "the American way" attempts to increase the prominence of multicultural perspectives in the curriculum. For instance, noted American historian Arthur Schlesinger, Jr. (1991a) warns us about where such an emphasis could lead: "But, pressed too far, the cult of ethnicity has unhealthy consequences. It gives rise, for example, to the conception of the U.S. as a nation composed not of individuals making their own choices but of inviolable ethnic and racial groups. It rejects the historic American goals of assimilation and integration. And, in an excess of zeal, well-intentioned people seek to transform our system of education from a means of creating 'one people' into a means of promoting, celebrating and perpetuating separate ethnic origins and identities. The balance is shifting from *unum* to *pluribus.*"

As the debate continues over how the education system should respond to the increasing demands made by the growing numbers of persons from different ethnic and cultural backgrounds in the American populace, the role of education will most certainly come under further scrutiny. If the role of education is to make a common culture of many cultures, then decisions will have to be made as to what will constitute that common culture. Deciding who will make those decisions and what the most effective means will be for ensuring input will nag the process until satisfactory answers are provided. Perhaps the opposing camps, which seem to have dug themselves in on either side of the issues involved, are not really sworn enemies but groups of clumsy and emotional opponents using different words to ask the same questions.

Understanding the Role of Graduate Education

The critical nature of graduate education is not generally understood. Graduate education sits at the top of the education pyramid, holding in one hand the promise of a better life for the recipient of the graduate degree, and, in the other, the expectation by the general public of leadership and expertise that result from concentrated study in a specific area. Universities always have worked diligently to fulfill this latter expectation, as they clearly demonstrated during the post-Sputnik period. But in accepting the challenge and the federal and private financial support to become the nation's leading research pioneers, universities were placed in a position to be affected by the public's perceptions of how well they were serving its needs. Derek Bok, president emeritus of Harvard University, has suggested that institutions of higher education are being "bashed these days . . . because they were not seen as taking part in a national agenda" (Mooney, 1992). In order to regain public support, "We must associate ourselves more prominently with solving the problems that concern Americans the most" (Mooney, 1992). In an increasingly culturally diverse nation, it is at least debatable how to reach consensus on what is of most concern. Institutions of higher education, then, may be most productive by providing the means to address the multitude of research interests and cultural perspectives that the changing graduate populations bring with them to the academy.

The traditional role of graduate education is the production of future scholars. Since 1977, institutions of higher education have produced a decreasing number of African American scholars. Ph.D.'s awarded to black graduate students dropped from 1,116 in 1977 to 828 in 1990 (National Research Council, 1990, p. 39). During the same period, universities managed to make only limited gains in the production of scholars from the nation's Hispanic and American Indian populations. There is abundant evidence that the reduction in the production of minority scholars, especially during the last ten years, poses a serious problem for higher education that will be felt most acutely during the early part of the twenty-first century. The national concern with this record of decreased production of Ph.D.'s by persons of color stems in part from a recognition of the need to address unattended parts of the "national agenda" to which Bok referred in the quote above. Those parts derive from the differences in perceptions among the various groups in society as to which "American problems" are unique to each of them, coupled with the realization that those problems may never be addressed by anyone except group members. The alienation that results spans the widest spectrum of societal activity and will increase with the expected growth of the nation's minority populations.

The attainment of a graduate degree provides entrance to and citizenship within the wider community of scholars. It validates one's contribution to the society of persons who produce new knowledge and maintain the standards of excellence associated with that production. The absence of large numbers of persons of color among this highly respected group of individuals not only serves to devalue the contributions that each nonwhite person might make to society but also, over time, indicts the intelligence and abilities of the entire group. Access to and participation in graduate education, then, are critical elements in any attempt to solve the problems of self-esteem that minority and underrepresented groups suffer in society.

Producing Minority Scholars

Several factors are involved in any effort to increase the number of nonwhite scholars. These include an understanding of the history of educational access and the problems involved in recruitment, admission, and retention of minorities in graduate school, as well as the influence of special support structures in the learning environment.

Legacy of Unequal Access. American education is a dynamic system undergoing constant change and development, adjusting both with the growth of knowledge and with the requirements placed on the system by changing societal needs. But throughout its history of reorganization, the education establishment has continued to be plagued by the legacy of discrimination and unequal access to quality education. Even after the 1954 Supreme Court decision in *Brown v. Board of Education,* conditions did not improve sufficiently for those who were previously underserved by the system to make a significant difference in their ability to find a place in the rapidly changing, increasingly technological workplace. After President Johnson signed Executive Order 11246 in 1965, laying the groundwork for affirmative action programs, education institutions were still unable to create a mechanism that would result in the effective preparation of the affected groups for full participation in the economic life of the nation. That inability still persists today. And that, today, is why we are still faced with the problem of finding ways to increase the production of minority scholars.

Recruitment, Admission, and Retention. In the last ten years, we have witnessed heightened concern over the problem of increasing the presence of minorities and women in graduate education. Almost all major universities now have programs in place to address the recruitment and admission of previously underrepresented students (Chandler and LaPidus, 1988). However, what has remained a surprisingly difficult problem is how to retain those students once they have been admitted. Faculties have, by and large, remained uninvolved in the process, and a recent study by People for the American Way reports that young people's perceptions about race relations have remained pessimistic (Collison, 1992). One result of the relative uninvolvement of faculty, reflected in the pessimism of the young, is that campus climates have remained uninviting to the newly admitted groups. Many believe that this factor has contributed to the high attrition rates of minority students. Claude Steele, a Stanford psychologist, has suggested that there is an additional culprit—"stigma" or "the endemic devaluation many blacks face in our society and schools" (1992, p. 68)—that adds to the difficulty of maintaining the minority presence.

Enrollment data reveal that an alarmingly high number of minority students are leaving our colleges and universities without completing their programs of study. Several reports document this phenomenon. According to Mason and Wharton (1990, p. 43), "71 percent of black 1980 high-school graduates and 66 percent of Hispanic graduates had left college by 1986 without a degree. By contrast, the rate of whites leaving without degrees was 55 percent."

Faculty Role. A major concern, shared by many who are seeking a solution to the problem of increasing the presence of minorities in graduate school, is how to get faculty more involved in the process of creating a supportive environment for minority students and faculty. A common premise in discussions of the problem is that the absence of active faculty involvement in attempts to enhance that presence may be a contributing factor to the resurgence of racial and ethnic hostilities on many of our nation's campuses. Graduate deans also have a role in the process because of their unique relationship with the faculty; deans touch their lives through the formal process of program review, and perhaps through the allocation of research or fellowship funds. In addition, deans interact with faculty in an informal way that is not available to administrators who control space, salaries, or advancement in rank. The graduate dean is often viewed as one who can cut across college and departmental lines, bringing issues that seriously affect graduate education to the attention of the faculty. Increased participation of minorities in graduate education, therefore, is one of the issues for which graduate deans can solicit the faculty's assistance. And the earlier faculty become involved in the process of identifying and recruiting minority students and faculty, the more cooperative they are likely to be in the effort to retain them.

The provision of incentives through additional research and teaching assistantships can involve entire departments in the process. Programs that require the matching of departmental and graduate school funds to support minority students who qualify for such merit-based support are very effective in gaining faculty and departmental commitment to these students. Such programs can form the basis of a broader range of support activity by the faculty.

At four-year institutions in the United States, an analysis of the racial composition of the faculty has indicated that it is still overwhelmingly white and male. Only 3 percent of the faculty is African American and only 2 percent is Hispanic (National Center for Education Statistics, 1990). Therefore, white male faculty must be at the forefront of the thrust to retain minority students and faculty in their programs. This effort calls for more than assurances that financial assistance will be available to the students. What must be accomplished in these academic settings is the effective crossing of racial barriers to develop lasting and mutually beneficial bonds between majority faculty and minority faculty and graduate students.

Graduate Teaching and Learning Environment. The contribution that an environment of support makes to the success of minority students, especially on predominantly white campuses, is demonstrated by the success of the Dorothy Danforth-Compton Fellows Program, which emphasizes this concept. Started in 1981, the program has produced nearly one hundred minority Ph.D.'s who are employed now at major universities throughout the country. It is implemented at ten institutions: Brown, Yale, University of Chicago, Columbia, Howard, Vanderbilt, University of Texas at Austin, University of California at Los Angeles, Stanford, and University of Washington.

Language of Encouragement. Several things work together to create a supportive environment for minority students. First, the institution in general and the departments in particular must develop a language of encouragement to communicate to all levels of the institution that the presence of minority students and faculty is neither the result of attempts to comply with federal regulations nor the implementation of lower academic standards. Presidents, chancellors, provosts, deans, and department chairs have an obligation to convey this message publicly and to educate their institution about their determination to assist in solving a problem that threatens the future of the nation. The language of encouragement also serves to reduce the hostility of the environment, making it more conducive to increased productivity and success for all concerned. When used by academic departments, this language clearly states to prospective graduate students the departments' admissions criteria and the relative weight of each criterion, and it conveys that the departments want to create a culturally diverse student body by addressing the needs of persons from groups that may have suffered previous discrimination.

Departmental Citizenship. Second, graduate departments must accord full departmental citizenship to all minority students and faculty. Full citizenship entails access to all rights and privileges available to all others in the same situation. One area that is cited frequently as exemplifying one's citizenship in a graduate department is whether one receives teaching and research assistantships. These assistantships facilitate close interaction between students and faculty, help students learn departmental regulations, and help them get a sense of the field. Two important mechanisms for developing self-assurance and skill as a graduate student are (1) meetings with other graduate assistants who teach the same class in order to discuss problems and plan teaching approaches and (2) evaluation by the faculty member whom the student assists. The support and constructive criticism of one's fellow research or teaching assistants sharpen academic skills and improve scholarship. Full citizenship means genuine consideration as a candidate for all of the positions and perquisites available to other graduate students in their respective programs.

Building Trust. Third is the necessity to convey to all faculty that their communication with minority graduate students is vital to the growth and well-being of their departments and the university as a whole. Many minority graduate students never become party to the informal information system that is a critical element in understanding the politics of individual departments. Without such information they run the risk of having the "wrong" dissertation adviser, of taking the "wrong" courses, and of forming the "wrong" dissertation or thesis committee. Information passed on from faculty to student in the informal information system is often the result of an evaluation by faculty of the student's ability to handle delicate matters and privileged information. This sensitive communication occurs as trust and respect develop between faculty and student. This mutual trust cannot be built without close and continual interaction in a variety of settings.

The role of the faculty is critical, for it is they who determine on a daily basis whether the students are in an atmosphere that supports their academic and social development. Often, the institution's reputation is communicated by its minority graduates to prospective applicants, and these opinions can be pivotal to decisions regarding the attractiveness of the institution. To a large extent, the nature of that reputation is in the hands of the faculty.

Who Is Responsible?

There is no guarantee that the problems outlined above can be solved either easily or in a relatively short time. Although it is the responsibility of the universities, colleges, and schools to find ways to educate the growing numbers of Asian Americans, African Americans, Hispanics, Native Americans, and immigrants who continue to be underserved by the education system, industry has an equal responsibility to provide them, once hired, with a work environment that will be conducive to their growth and development, that will respect and reward their contributions, and that will support the realization of their full potential. The practice of bringing more minorities into the workplace is necessary, but not sufficient, for the creation of a diverse work force. The quantitative change has to be accompanied by a qualitative change in the work environment so as to breed excellence, teamwork, and pride in product.

The general role of education and the particular role of public universities in keeping the nation competitive are very clear, but the burden is not exclusively theirs. As Bok has pointed out, "Universities may not have any special capacity to prescribe solutions to the nation's ills. But they are better equipped than any other institution to produce the knowledge needed to arrive at effective solutions and to prepare the highly educated people required to carry them out" (Magner, 1990). The solution may reside in a working partnership between industry and education, on the one hand, and state and federal governments, on the other, to provide the sustained support required to change the conditions that perpetuate and compound the current problems.

Industry is one of the major beneficiaries of a well-educated population, and partnerships with the business and industrial sector can be critical to the success of ventures to enhance the educational preparation of students. There are several linkages already existing between universities and industry, especially at those research institutions where there is a great deal of technology transfer taking place. Massachusetts Institute of Technology, Carnegie-Mellon, California Institute of Technology, and University of Washington are examples that immediately come to mind. But states, too, are engaged in facilitating these partnerships, including the Edison Program in Ohio, the Ben Franklin Program in Pennsylvania, and the programs coordinated through the Western Interstate Commission for Higher Education (Odell and Mock, 1989).

Recommendations

One of the persistent remnants of racial prejudice and previously legalized discrimination in the United States is an overarching presence of racism in its many and varied forms in our daily lives. While, on the one hand, this racism exists, there is, on the other, a history of genuine and constant attempts to nullify the dysfunctional and arguably harmful effects that race-related activities have had on our society. These activities now touch all aspects of our lives and are manifested on a daily basis in the ways in which we think, talk, feel, and act; where and how we live; where we work and what we do there; where we go to school and what we learn. Today, our education institutions are in the midst of yet another period of reevaluation and readjustment of their mission, prompted largely by questions springing from their responsibility to educate the general population to live in an ethnically and racially diverse society, and from their failure to educate the minorities who make up an increasingly larger percentage of our population.

The discussions of how to remedy this situation have resulted in a number of initiatives, both publicly and institutionally supported, designed to enhance the recruitment and retention of persons of color to the nation's campuses (Green, 1989; Chandler and LaPidus, 1988, 1992). But as a by-product of these discussions, many institutions find that much more is needed than just a change in the numerical ratios among the various campus populations if the presence of minorities is to be maintained and enhanced.

Use Diversity to Enhance Quality. What makes the notion of diversity attractive is that it provides institutions of higher learning with a low-cost mechanism to incorporate the talents and to benefit from the contributions of all persons on the campus. Diversity is internally driven, springing from an institutional interest in maintaining the quality of its product in the face of a changing work force and student body. In this regard, the academy is not unlike industry, where the concern is to remain competitive on both the national and international levels. The current practice of institutionalized denial of the contributions that women and persons of color make to the academy at all levels results in the continued underutilization of our population and is maintained at an enormous cost. How costly is it to a campus when it suffers disruptions because it is perceived to be insensitive to the needs of all students, or to turn a deaf ear to complaints of sexist or racist acts committed by its faculty, staff, or students? How much more costly is it when alumni recognize that their education did not prepare them for the kind of society in which they must forge a living? Although diversity does not guarantee that sexist or racist acts will cease in society at large, it certainly holds the promise that these acts will be drastically reduced in a work force that is sensitive to the needs of a wide variety of groups and individuals. In the end, universities must find ways to ensure that as the racial, cultural, and ethnic compositions of their campuses change, they not only maintain the quality and level of productivity for which they are known but also seize whatever opportunities the added diversity provides to enhance their productivity and improve their excellence.   257047

Go Beyond Numbers. The urgency and importance of going beyond numbers become more critical as we witness the resurgence of overtly racist and sexist acts on many of our predominantly white campuses, including the University of Michigan, University of Massachusetts at Amherst, Stanford University, University of Texas at Austin, and University of Southern California. According to a survey conducted by Walter Allen, a University of Michigan sociologist, "Four out of five blacks reported experiencing some form of racial discrimination" at the sixteen predominantly white colleges in the sample (Wilkerson, 1988). Also, according to the National Institute Against Prejudice and Violence, "At least three hundred campuses have experienced incidents of harassment and violence involving race, religion, ethnicity, or sexual orientation since it began keeping track of such conflicts in 1986" (Magner, 1990). But this resurgence is more disturbing because it is coupled with an outbreak of even more violent racially motivated crimes in society at large. This "air of intolerance" comes at the very time that the numbers of students from African American, Chicano and Latino, and American Indian backgrounds who are seeking advanced degrees at our nation's academic institutions are beginning to show slight increases over what they were in the last decade (Magner, 1991).

Make the Campus Climate Welcoming. As we search for a means to create a truly diverse campus community, we are faced immediately with a series of questions. What would be the characteristics of such a campus? How would we know when we have achieved such a state? Are there campuses or communities that we can identify as models or guides? How could we modify our current policies and practices to enable us to attain the goal of diversity? Will a diverse campus do irreparable harm to the current rate of our productivity, our quality, and our scholarship? These and other questions are important as we try to translate our commitment to diversity into action, and our dream of achieving that goal into a reality.

Diversity, as the term is used in this context, takes us beyond the concerns about access and the preoccupation with numbers. It requires us to look into the institution, where questions pertaining to institutional climate, to the quality of the work environment, to collegiality, and to equity are addressed. It takes us to places where hidden barriers and invisible personal boundaries make their subtle but undeniable appearance. It gives us a tool to begin the process of changing our responses to some of our most deeply embedded cues. It prompts us to make programmatic changes that comply with, but differ significantly from, the current structure of our institution, and it challenges us to take individual and institutional risks while we try both to accommodate our private beliefs and to confront our private prejudices.

No environment can be made totally free of factors that can alienate individuals who must operate within it. The factors that produce alienation sometimes are unfortunately exaggerated as we bring together into the limited space called the university people from different cultural, economic, and social backgrounds. But as institutions make a conscious effort to remove barriers that impede the progress of their growing numbers of new citizens, they will make it possible for individuals to confront and conquer their private fears. What more critical role can there be for education as we prepare for the twenty-first century?

References

Chandler, T. L., and LaPidus, J. B. *Enhancing the Minority Presence in Graduate Education.* Vol. 1. Washington, D.C.: Council of Graduate Schools, 1988.

Chandler, T. L., and LaPidus, J. B. *Enhancing the Minority Presence in Graduate Education.* Vol. 2: *Assessing Progress.* Washington, D.C.: Council of Graduate Schools, 1992.

Collison, M. "Young People Found Pessimistic About Relations Between the Races." *Chronicle of Higher Education,* March 25, 1992, p. A1.

D'Souza, D. *Illiberal Education: The Politics of Sex and Race on Campus.* New York: Free Press, 1991.

Finn, C. E., Jr. "Why Can't Colleges Convey Our Diverse Culture's Unifying Themes?" *Chronicle of Higher Education,* June 13, 1990, p. A40.

Green, M. F. (ed.). *Minorities on Campus: A Handbook for Enhancing Diversity.* Washington, D.C.: American Council on Education, 1989.

Magner, D. K. "Racial Tensions Continue to Erupt on Campuses Despite Efforts to Promote Cultural Diversity." *Chronicle of Higher Education,* June 6, 1990, p. A29.

Magner, D. K. "Hispanics Remain Grossly Underrepresented on Campus, Report Says." *Chronicle of Higher Education,* January 23, 1991, p. A2.

Mason, S. C., and Wharton, C. R., Jr. *Three Realities: Minority Life in the United States.* Washington, D.C.: Business-Higher Education Forum, 1990.

Mooney, C. J. "Bok: To Avoid Bashing, Colleges Must Take a Leadership Role on National Problems." *Chronicle of Higher Education,* April 8, 1992, p. A17.

National Center for Education Statistics. *Faculty in Higher Education Institutions, 1988.* Washington, D.C.: Government Printing Office, 1990.

National Commission on Excellence in Education. *A Nation at Risk: The Imperative for Educational Reform.* Washington, D.C.: National Commission on Excellence in Education, 1983.

National Research Council. *Summary Report, 1990: Doctorate Recipients from United States Universities.* Washington, D.C.: National Research Council, 1990.

Odell, M., and Mock, J. J. (eds.). *A Crucial Agenda: Making Colleges and Universities Work Better for Minority Students.* Boulder, Colo.: Western Interstate Commission for Higher Education, 1989.

Schlesinger, A. M., Jr. "The Cult of Ethnicity, Good or Bad." *Time,* July 8, 1991a, p. 21.

Schlesinger, A. M., Jr. *The Disuniting of America.* Knoxville, Tenn.: Whittle Books, 1991b.

Steele, C. "Race and the Schooling of Black Americans." *Atlantic Monthly,* April 1992, pp. 68–78.

Steele, S. *The Content of Our Character.* New York: St. Martin's Press, 1990a.

Steele, S. " 'I'm Black, You're White, Who's Innocent?' Race and Power in an Era of Blame." *Harper's Magazine,* June 1990b, pp. 45–51.

Wilkerson, I. "Campus Blacks Feel Racism's Nuances." *New York Times,* April 17, 1988, p. 1.

TREVOR L. CHANDLER *is assistant vice chancellor for campus diversity at the University of California, Davis. He was previously associate dean of the graduate school at the University of Washington and dean-in-residence at the Council of Graduate Schools.*

If a broader conception of scholarship can be incorporated into graduate education and if colleges and universities will hire and reward the graduates of those programs, new faculty will be better prepared for their work.

Openness to a Broader View of Scholarship

Laurie Richlin

The disparity between the graduate research training that creates the Ph.D.'s who become the next generation of faculty and the need for those new faculty to be able to make connections among disciplines, to inform their research with practice, and, most important, to teach has led to increased dissatisfaction among the deans and department chairs who hire them. While one necessary step in achieving this needed diversity of scholarship is to change the institutional and departmental reward systems to encourage different interests, that change alone is not sufficient. To meet the need for teacher-scholars, the faculty of the future must be composed of people interested in and able to meet the challenges of a broader definition of scholarship. This change has not been achieved, and cannot be achieved, by continuing with "business as usual" in doctoral programs. If we select only people who will fit into the narrow tube of graduate education, tell them that only a narrow range of activities is valuable in their disciplines, and educate them within the confines of a narrow conception of scholarship, they will be unable to contribute to the diversity of scholarships that we seek. Those undergraduate students who self-select to continue with graduate education currently expect that their experience will be narrow in scope and that they, too, will need to find small areas of specialization in order to complete their doctorates. (As described by the Council of Graduate Schools [1991], in some fields the topics and methodologies may even be chosen for the students by the principal researchers for whom they work.) Certainly, the large majority of faculty who never publish anything during their careers except that which comes out of their dissertation research demonstrate how

NEW DIRECTIONS FOR TEACHING AND LEARNING, no. 54, Summer 1993   © Jossey-Bass Publishers

little the interest in pure discovery scholarship is among those who are forced to do it to obtain the "union card." Even with departmental reward systems designed to encourage a wide range of faculty activities, if graduate students, the faculty of the future, are not selected, motivated, and educated to do other than narrow discovery-type research, that work will not be done. To cultivate a diverse faculty, we need to begin at the beginning.

Attempts to provide teaching experience and information have been piecemeal add-ons, either as part of the teaching assistantship in graduate school or in faculty development programs at the employing institution. As Glazer (this volume) discusses, the Doctor of Arts (D.A.) degree, established to provide a graduate program designed specifically to prepare college teachers within the disciplines, did not obtain the respect and resulting success that its originators had hoped for. There is no hope of resuscitating the D.A. at this point. Rather, it will be necessary to work within the accepted Ph.D. format in each discipline.

A Study of Institutional Openness to a Broader View of Scholarship

Success in encouraging graduate students to work in the variety of scholarship categories depends on the willingness of doctorate-granting departments to award the Ph.D. for alternative doctoral programs and the willingness of departments to hire graduates of those programs. In order to find out how open doctoral programs (the "providers") and departments in non-doctorate-granting schools (the "consumers") are to the alternative scholarships, I sent 1,219 questionnaires to deans of graduate studies (providers) and academic deans (consumers), and to chairs of departments of biology, history, mathematics, and psychology at 251 U.S. colleges and universities (Richlin, 1991). Providers were in Carnegie classifications (see Carnegie Foundation for the Advancement of Teaching, 1987) Research University 1, Research University 2, and Doctorate Granting 1 and Doctorate Granting 2; consumers were in Carnegie classifications Comprehensive 1, Comprehensive 2, Liberal Arts 1, and Liberal Arts 2. Public and private institutions were chosen in proportion to their numbers within each category. (Doctorate-granting institutions in the sample also employ newly minted Ph.D.'s, of course, but faculty responsibilities at those institutions are likely to be skewed more in the direction of research scholarship than of undergraduate teaching. Also, asking the same respondent about providing an alternate doctoral program *and* hiring the graduates might well have muddied the responses.)

Completed surveys were returned by 630 people (51.7 percent), including 270 (51.5 percent) providers and 360 (51.8 percent) consumers. One hundred (15.9 percent) of the 630 respondents were women, 75 percent of them in the consumer institutions. The great majority of respondents (96.7

percent) held Ph.D.'s; 96.6 percent of providers and 77.5 percent of consumers received their highest degrees from research universities; over 60 percent of providers obtained their degrees in the 1950s and 1960s, while over 60 percent of consumers were awarded their degrees in the 1970s and 1980s.

The chairs and deans were presented with four different outlines of possible Ph.D. programs. The different programs had the same coursework, focused on disciplinary knowledge and leading to qualifying examinations. What differed among the program types was the kind of scholarship that the students used for their dissertations, which were described (following Boyer, 1990) as follows: (1) *discovery:* the search for new facts, creation of new knowledge and new theory in a disciplinary specialization; (2) *integration:* synthesis of disparate views and information in a disciplinary specialization; (3) *application:* reflection on practice, creation of new paradigms of professional competence; and (4) *teaching:* representation of knowledge, creation of new ways to draw the field together to connect knower and learner.

Results: Willingness to Grant the Degree or Hire the Graduates

Providers were asked whether they would award the Ph.D. for each dissertation type, and consumers were asked their likelihood of hiring graduates of the corresponding program. Responses of willingness to grant or hire are shown in Table 10.1.

Discovery. For the traditional discovery orientation, there was almost total agreement among providers that they would grant the doctorate. Among consumers, however, there was less agreement, with the numbers declining along the Carnegie classification continuum. Obviously, many departments had not found the hiring of faculty with a strict research orientation to be useful for their campuses.

Integration. Providers were much less willing to award the Ph.D. for integration dissertations than they were for the discovery type. Barely over half of the Research 1 universities said they would do so, with slightly more of the other providers willing to hire. On the other hand, consumers were very open to hiring Ph.D.'s with integration scholarship, with all categories over 80 percent.

Application. Providers were even less willing to grant the Ph.D. for application-oriented dissertations. There was considerable interest among consumers, however, in hiring graduates with application scholarship. Except for the more selective (Liberal Arts 1) colleges, over 75 percent of consumers indicated a willingness to hire.

Pedagogy. The greatest difference between providers and consumers was apparent in the area of pedagogical scholarship. Approximately 66 percent of provider department chairs and deans said they would not award the Ph.D. for dissertations done on the way in which knowledge in their fields was taught or learned. Consumers, however, showed considerable

Table 10.1. Percentages of Respondents
Willing to Grant Ph.D. for or to Hire Graduates
of Alternative Ph.D. Programs

Institutional Type	Program Type			
	Discovery	Integration	Application	Pedagogy
Providers				
Research 1	100	52.2	43.5	35.6
Research 2	100	61.1	57.0	26.4
Doctorate-Granting 1 and 2	99.0	73.5	51.4	36.6
All	99.6	64.5	50.2	33.4
Consumers				
Comprehensive 1	94.4	94.5	80.0	65.6
Comprehensive 2	92.1	93.3	84.1	70.7
Liberal Arts 1	85.7	85.8	62.6	49.4
Liberal Arts 2	84.2	84.0	76.0	82.7
All	90.0	89.6	75.6	66.3

Note: Provider institutions are those willing to grant Ph.D.'s for alternative Ph.D. programs, and consumer institutions are those willing to hire graduates of the programs. The typology of institutions is based on Carnegie Foundation for the Advancement of Teaching, 1987.

interest in hiring Ph.D.'s with pedagogical scholarship. Once again, except for respondents at the more selective liberal arts schools, more than 66 percent of consumers were open to hiring graduates of this type of program.

The information reported by consumers in this study clearly shows that there is a need for Ph.D.'s better prepared in their graduate programs to integrate material within their respective disciplines and across other disciplines, provide service through application of theory to real problems, and to become college teachers able to cover a wide variety of material. With the anticipated replacement of approximately 340,000 faculty members during the next fifteen years, and the problems already being reported by some sectors (and expected by all) in finding qualified college teachers, it is evident that there are (and will continue to be) positions waiting for Ph.D.'s whose dissertation research is concerned with how to transmit disciplinary knowledge to undergraduates. Unlike the D.A., the pedagogically based Ph.D. program would fulfill (and be perceived as fulfilling) the same high scholarly requirements associated with traditional disciplinary Ph.D.'s. But this fulfillment will require the establishment of pedagogy as an intellectual activity, which is, as Shulman (1990) has said, "very tightly coupled to scholarship in the disciplines themselves."

Recommendations for Faculty and Administrators

Contrary to Berelson's (1960) belief that the liberal arts colleges are responsible for buying researchers and retraining them as teachers, the primary theme of this volume is that graduate programs must be encouraged to help future faculty develop a wide range of scholarly abilities. This theme is at the heart of the following recommendations.

Design Graduate Programs to Encourage a Diverse Range of Scholarly Talents. The next important intellectual task for the reflective practitioners among the graduate faculty is to design programs to educate the faculty of the future in their specific disciplines, the connections among disciplines, the wisdom of practice, and the pedagogy of their disciplines. New visions of scholarship depend on models of graduate education that will attract and inspire our best and brightest undergraduates to pursue academic careers, bringing and developing their own ways of thinking. As suggested by the authors in this volume, graduate programs must tie coursework to the dissertation, encourage collaborative work, get students and faculty out of the academy and into the field, and promote scholarly teaching through developmentally based programs.

Continue to Explore What Scholarship Can Be in Each Discipline. Beyond individual effort, we need to reconceptualize how content-based knowledge and "knowing" work within the disciplines. What does it mean to make teaching an intellectual activity in history? How similar to or different from the same effort is it in mathematics? What does "thinking like a psychologist" mean? How do we teach students how to do it? What are the barriers to learning in the different fields? These and other questions vital to education will only begin to be answered when faculty define what a wide diversity of scholarship looks like.

Reward a Diverse Range of Scholarly Talents and Activities. The last great service that the retiring faculty can render for the future of American higher education is to set in place the reward systems needed to recognize and encourage more diverse scholarship in the academy. My study of deans and department chairs, reported above, once again highlighted the fact that the reward structure is tied more to the characteristics of the institution than to any specific discipline (Richlin, 1991). Fine arts faculty may operate differently from science faculty to a certain degree, but each operates within the bounds of the institution's mission, and the type of scholarship valued comes from the institutional promotion and tenure system. Ways recommended by the authors of this volume to encourage more diversity in scholarly activity include credit for jointly authored papers and team-taught classes, recognition of the application of theory (for instance, by education faculty in the local school district or by engineering faculty in an environmental effort) as scholarship, and acceptance as scholarship those articles or books that use up-to-date pedagogical theory as a basis for better learning in the discipline.

Conclusion

As Schuster (this volume) writes, only the graduate school, with its influence on graduate programs, has the legitimacy, familiarity, and modulated role to fill the leadership vacuum in addressing issues of preparation for the professoriate. Our challenge is to provide a large enough number of well-prepared faculty to replace those who are retiring over the next twenty years and to ensure that the new faculty are the highest quality possible, bringing into the professoriate as wide a range of backgrounds and experience as possible.

References

Berelson, B. *Graduate Education in the United States.* New York: McGraw-Hill, 1960.

Boyer, E. L. *Scholarship Reconsidered: Priorities of the Professoriate.* Princeton, N.J.: Princeton University Press, 1990.

Carnegie Foundation for the Advancement of Teaching. *A Classification of Institutions of Higher Education.* Princeton, N.J.: Princeton University Press, 1987.

Council of Graduate Schools. *The Role and Nature of the Doctoral Dissertation.* Washington, D.C.: Council of Graduate Schools, 1991.

Richlin, L. "Preparing Future Faculty: Meeting the Need for Teacher-Scholars by Enlarging the View of Scholarship in Ph.D. Programs." Unpublished doctoral dissertation, Department of Education, Claremont Graduate School, 1991.

Shulman, L. S. "The New American Scholar: A Teacher of Substance." Address presented at the Scholarship of Teaching Conference, Iona College, New Rochelle, New York, October 1990.

LAURIE RICHLIN is interim director of the Office of Research and Evaluation Studies, Antioch College, Yellow Springs, Ohio. She is also executive editor of the Journal on Excellence in College Teaching *and director of the Lilly Conference on College Teaching–West.*

INDEX

109

ORDERING INFORMATION

NEW DIRECTIONS FOR TEACHING AND LEARNING is a series of paperback books that presents ideas and techniques for improving college teaching, based both on the practical expertise of seasoned instructors and on the latest research findings of educational and psychological researchers. Books in the series are published quarterly in Spring, Summer, Fall, and Winter and are available for purchase by subscription and individually.

SUBSCRIPTIONS for 1993 cost $45.00 for individuals (a savings of 25 percent over single-copy prices) and $60.00 for institutions, agencies, and libraries. Please do not send institutional checks for personal subscriptions. Standing orders are accepted.

SINGLE COPIES cost $14.95 when payment accompanies order. (California, New Jersey, New York, and Washington, D.C., residents please include appropriate sales tax.) Billed orders will be charged postage and handling.

DISCOUNTS FOR QUANTITY ORDERS are available. Please write to the address below for information.

ALL ORDERS must include either the name of an individual or an official purchase order number. Please submit your order as follows:
   Subscriptions: specify series and year subscription is to begin
   Single copies: include individual title code (such as TL1)

MAIL ALL ORDERS TO:
   Jossey-Bass Publishers
   350 Sansome Street
   San Francisco, California 94104

FOR SINGLE-COPY SALES OUTSIDE OF THE UNITED STATES CONTACT:
   Maxwell Macmillan International Publishing Group
   866 Third Avenue
   New York, New York 10022

FOR SUBSCRIPTION SALES OUTSIDE OF THE UNITED STATES, contact any international subscription agency or Jossey-Bass directly.